WHAT COLLEGE TRUSTEES NEED TO KNOW

WHAT COLLEGE TRUSTEES NEED TO KNOW

Important Questions Sometimes Asked Too Late ... Or Never at All

by

GEORGE J. MATTHEWS
CHAIRMAN EMERITUS, NORTHEASTERN UNIVERSITY

NORMAN R. SMITH
PRESIDENT EMERITUS, WAGNER COLLEGE

BRYAN E. CARLSON
PRESIDENT, CES/REGISTRY FOR COLLEGE & UNIVERSITY PRESIDENTS

iUniverse, Inc.
Bloomington

WHAT COLLEGE TRUSTEES NEED TO KNOW
IMPORTANT QUESTIONS SOMETIMES ASKED
TO LATE...OR NEVER AT ALL

iUniverse books may be ordered through booksellers or by contacting:

iUniverse
1663 Liberty Drive
Bloomington, IN 47403
www.iuniverse.com
1-800-Authors (1-800-288-4677)

Because of the dynamic nature of the Internet, any web addresses or links contained in this book may have changed since publication and may no longer be valid. The views expressed in this work are solely those of the author and do not necessarily reflect the views of the publisher, and the publisher hereby disclaims any responsibility for them.

Any people depicted in stock imagery provided by Thinkstock are models, and such images are being used for illustrative purposes only.

Certain stock imagery © Thinkstock.

ISBN: 978-1-4759-8150-6 (hc)

Library of Congress Control Number: 2013905366

Printed in the United States of America

iUniverse rev. date: 3/13/2013

DEDICATION

To

Caroline Robinson Smith
Skidmore College Class of 2014

Kathleen Waters Matthews

Dr. Edward. W. Carlson

CHAPTERS

Acknowledgments

W e gratefully salute the following friends, colleagues and spouses who contributed their wise counsel during the writing of this book. Registry Vice Presidents Amy Lauren Miller and Kevin Matthews, and Holly Dellacanonica are inspirations for their commitment, wisdom, and professional spirit. Dr. Susan Robinson, currently part of the founding senior management team of AVENUES The World School, lent her extensive expertise in admissions and financial aid along with her broader wise counsel emanating from a distinguished career in higher education and the arts. Anne Carlson's support and patience is gratefully acknowledged, especially her tolerance of far too many pre-dawn sessions working through the many chapters of this book.

George J. Matthews was Chairman of the

Northeastern University Board of Trustees from 1989 to 1999, a decade when Northeastern evolved from a regional institution to a widely-acclaimed and sought-after top-ranked national university. Today, Matthews is the founding Chairman of Collegiate Enterprise Solutions and the Chancellor of the venerable Registry for College and University Presidents, comprising over 420 highly successful veteran CEO's Provost, Deans and other senior executives who provide interim leadership for higher education institutions seeking outside expertise when senior level vacancies occur. Over the past 20 years since its founding, the Registry has provided 345 interim placements to over 270 institutions. Matthews is also co-founder of the Club of Madrid, located in Madrid, Spain, and dedicated to fostering democracy worldwide. Ninety former presidents and prime ministers, from countries throughout the world, form its membership.

Norman R. Smith is President Emeritus of

Wagner College in New York, where during his 14 year tenure,
the College evolved from bottom tier ranking and near
bankruptcy, to capacity enrollment, continuous fiscal stability,
record fund raising, and top tier ranking. Smith went on to be
President of Richmond The American International University in
London, England and then became Founding Chancellor and
architect of what was to be the largest American international
university in the world, on the Egyptian Mediterranean shore
west of Alexandria. That project ended following the Egyptian
revolution. Earlier in his career, he was Assistant Dean of two
Harvard University graduate schools: Education and then the
John F. Kennedy School of Government. His last book, TOP TIER
The Wagner College Turnaround Years, was cited as a "Book of
Note for College Presidents" by the Council of Independent
Colleges. He is presently affiliated with the Registry and has
worked in partnership consultations with George Matthews.

Bryan E. Carlson is the President of the

Registry for College and University Presidents and the founding
President of Collegiate Enterprise Solutions (CES). From 1976 to
1999, he was President of Mount Ida College in Massachusetts,
where he led the College through an extraordinary era of
consistent growth, transformation, and financial success. Over
the past decade, he has overseen the Registry's evolution into
having become the preeminent interim executive leadership firm
in the nation. During that time, CES and the Registry have had
over 400 engagements with colleges and universities nationwide
and internationally for either consultation or interim leadership.
Carlson is also the former President and CEO of the New England
Exchange for Executive Leadership (NEXEL), and was the
founding President of the College Bound Selection Service.

Introduction

This book was written with the recognition that most Trustees are very busy people and are probably extending themselves beyond reasonable expectation by taking on the voluntary, and noble, responsibility of serving as a college Trustee. Because of the demands placed upon them, most Trustees really don't have endless amounts of time to be reading about the complexities of every facet of higher education. Respecting that, we have tried to focus this book on those key dimensions and measurements that are not only critical to the viability of most colleges, but, to our surprise and concern, often not sufficiently understood by many Trustees.

Our CES/Registry of College and University Presidents consultations spanning hundreds of colleges and universities have given us the opportunity to work closely with Trustees throughout the country. From these experiences, we have accumulated a collection of essentials that we have found to be most frequently in need of greater Trustee awareness.

This book is not intended to be a comprehensive encyclopedia or scholarly research report. The many professional educational associations in the US, from the Association of Governing Boards (AGB) to the Council of Independent Colleges (CIC), all have publishing entities that annually issue voluminous collections of books and articles that report higher education issues in much greater detail and depth.

You'll likely notice pretty quickly that we have deliberately elected to write this book as if we were having a conversation with you. The tone is colloquial and, we hope, reader friendly. The chapters are short and, we hope, engaging and readable. The intent is candor. The method is getting to the point and not getting lost in unnecessary detail or burdensome jargon-ese.

We hope that no more than a few readers will be annoyed that we have repeated key tenets, and clichés, with the intent of driving home what we consider to be the most essential points of the book. We hope you don't groan too much when you come across such "echoes."

The title of this book is **WHAT COLLEGE TRUSTEES NEED TO KNOW** with an emphasis on 'KNOW' and therefore should not be construed as advising College Trustees to "DO." Much has been written that justly delineates the role of the Board vs. the role of the Chief Executive Officer. Too often, college Boards of Trustees have been known to over-reach their role and meddle in the management of the institution. Such conduct invariably impairs the ability of the chief executive to have the authority necessary to manage effectively.

This book has no intention of inciting Boards to take over the authority of the chief executive. **However, Boards do have a fiduciary responsibility, simply put, to know what is going on,** especially at troubled institutions facing declines and shortages. Should the bottom drop out, it is the Trustees and the CEO whose names will be listed on all the lawsuits. . .not faculty, staff, and the many other constituencies who expect a role in the 'shared governance' of the institution.

This book hopefully helps Trustees better understand what they need to know in order to ask the right questions and, in doing so, perhaps nip potential crises in the bud before more drastic interventions become necessary.

Beyond that, the classic tenets of the Board role remain intact.

If the book's title conveys the impression that College Trustees are typically being misled or otherwise deliberately misinformed, that would be an unfortunate misperception.

Rather, this book simply recognizes, from observed case study experiences, that far too many Trustees, especially at smaller colleges, appear to know very little about the way in which colleges are managed and even less about the vital signs that can make or break a college.

Most college Trustees, after all, are not educators and have never worked in a higher educational environment. Board meetings aren't designed to teach the basics of higher education management and often proceed at a brisk pace that assumes each Trustee has an in depth knowledge of the fundamentals, and sometimes the fine detail.

This book, therefore, aspires to equip Trustees with the basics, especially those basics essential to the vital functions of the institution. In being so equipped, hopefully the readers will be in a stronger position to make the positive contributions that are sought from all Trustees.

On that positive note, the authors wish to emphasize how essential it is that any successful college has a Board of

Trustees and Senior Administration that are working hand-in-hand and thereby rowing in the same direction toward a mutually agreed-upon destination. This teamwork starts at the top with the Board Chairman and the President, each of whom have a responsibility, in turn, to build that same spirit of common good and cooperation within the constituencies they oversee.

There is no question that even the best ideas, and the most perfect aspirations, for a college cannot be achieved when the people affected by the goal, and especially those responsible for its execution, don't believe in the direction and, even worse, hope that the journey fails. Such failure is virtually assured when too many key players haven't bought in and aren't on board.

That is not to say, though, that Trustees should acquiesce and accept everything management presents without asking questions that challenge management to aim high and to confront problems and issues realistically. The eclectic expertise that a Board of Trustees comprises should be viewed as an asset, and as a resource that should be tapped and welcomed. But, to truly be a valuable resource, Trustees need to understand the fundamentals and recognize the nature of problems typical to the institution they are overseeing.

Small, enrollment-revenue dependent colleges are facing the most daunting problems

of their entire existence. Colleges and universities
that overcome their challenges and flourish will be those
where Trustees, management and faculty are working on
each others' behalf toward a common cause. They may not
always agree on every detail, and may sometimes disagree
on what some consider key issues.

**But, all the key players and most notably
Trustees, management and faculty, absolutely
have to end up buying into and working toward
the same purpose if the institution has any hope
of moving on to higher plateaus, or even staying
alive.**

At the end of this book is a brief summary of bullet
points extracted from previous chapters, and is thereby
intended as a reference list of questions you need to be
asking at Board meetings when presented with information
about institutional performance.

We hope you'll find our 'conversation' with you
engaging, enlightening and worth your time. Let us know?

GEORGE J. MATTHEWS
NORMAN R. SMITH
BRYAN E. CARLSON

Chapter 1

Defining the Audience
& Rationale for this Book

The Carnegie Commission, which classifies colleges and universities in the US, cites about 4,400 higher education institutions nationwide which collectively enroll about 17.5 million students. Of these 4,400 institutions, *The Chronicle of Higher Education's* 2012 Almanac lists 3,418 as non-profit. These non-profit institutions divide almost equally among those that are state-supported and those that are independent, and therefore heavily dependent on enrollment revenues.

Most college undergraduates, nearly 80%, are
enrolled in approximately 1,705 government-subsidized
public universities like the SUNY system in New York State
and the UCal/CSU system in California. The remaining 20%
or so, about 3.8 million undergraduate students, are enrolled
in the 1,713 non-government subsidized colleges and
universities typically called either private or independent.
Thus, eight out of ten college students are enrolled in that
half of the institutions that are public supported.

In the 1960's, now more than 50 years ago, over two-
thirds of all college students attended independent colleges
and universities. Since that baby boom college decade, there
has been a massive shift away from independent colleges
and toward state institutions for one inherently obvious
reason: lower tuition rates offered by the massive number of
more-affordable state universities that have been created
over the past half century.

Not surprisingly, the highest concentration of smaller,
tuition-dependent colleges is in the East, most established
before the 20th century, and many founded by churches.
Even Harvard, in the 1600's, started as a divinity college.
As tabulated in the 2012-13 *Chronicle of Higher Education*
Annual Almanac, nearly 350 of the 1,713 independent, non-
profit colleges and universities in the US are in just three
states, New York, Pennsylvania and Massachusetts. While
California is also heavily populated with over 140
independent colleges, most western states, because of their

2

relative age, are largely public university domains.
Collectively, these four states account for nearly one-third
of all independent colleges and universities nationwide.
Wyoming is without an independent small college and Alaska
has but one.

Of the 1,713 private/independent institutions, about
110 are major research universities including Harvard, Yale,
and Stanford. Also included within the independent group
are some very wealthy smaller colleges like Swarthmore,
Wellesley, Williams and Pomona Colleges. While even the
largest and richest of independent colleges and universities
are also meaningfully financially dependent on tuition
revenues, this book doesn't directly address their issues and,
as such, they are not counted as enrollment-revenue, or
tuition, dependent.

Among these 1,713 private colleges and universities,
again as tabulated in the *Chronicle's* 2012-13 Almanac,
13% or about 220 enjoy endowments of at least $250
million. 'Only' five universities of those 220 have over $12
billion each (Harvard leads with over twice that amount)
. . .56 have endowments of at least $1 billion. . .and another
60 report over $500 million.

In today's economy, the amount of revenue typically
drawn from endowment is not likely to exceed 5%, if that.
So, even a seemingly impressive $500 million endowment
isn't sufficient as it likely contributes little more than

$20 million to an annual operating budget that is probably at least five times larger, thereby leaving even 'comfortably endowed' institutions also largely dependent on annual enrollment revenues.

This book is directed to Trustees of the nearly 90% of independent colleges and universities, about 1,500, with even smaller endowments than the top 220 that have $500 million or more.

As such, these 1,500 colleges are essentially _totally_ enrollment revenue dependent. . .and will likely remain that way for decades to come, if not forever. Their survival, or certainly their viability, calls upon them to be increasingly more focused on doing what is necessary to enroll students who are capable of paying a substantial tuition rate that far exceeds what they would be paying in a public university. . . which is why nearly 80% of all college students are not enrolled in tuition-revenue dependent colleges.

Even among those 1,500 colleges, there may likely be ones for which this book has not been written.

"If it isn't broken, don't fix it" is a fair-enough tenet. **In that spirit, this book may not resonate with those Trustees who oversee colleges where. . .**

4

- the annual operating budget is consistently balanced without seriously denying critical operating expenses, including physical plant, planned maintenance and salaries.

- enrollment goals are consistently met and even exceeded.

- at least 40% of those students who applied and were offered admission accepted the admit offer and enrolled.

- at least 60% of those students who enrolled subsequently stated that they had opted for their first choice institution.

- at least 70% or more of those students originally enrolled graduate.

- the retention rate from freshman to sophomore year exceeds 90%.
- discounting (i.e., unfunded, un-endowed grants) is below 30% of gross tuition revenues.

- no more than 25% of annual donations realized is being spent on fundraising costs.

- **all academic majors being offered have at least 25 majors in each of the junior and senior years.**

Yes, all of the above are **quantifiably measureable** performance outcomes comparable to criteria employed when assessing any business for its success. Enrollment-revenue dependent colleges have no choice but to actually focus on generating enrollment-revenue. No matter how wonderful the academic program, it doesn't matter all that much if the bills can't get paid.

Contrary to what many academicians would like to believe, colleges have to employ fundamental business sensibilities when making operational decisions, including those directly affecting the academic programs being offered. Especially among the 1,500 tuition dependent colleges for which this book has been written, the realization that a very large number of colleges are competing for a very small portion of the college student population requires all such colleges to face tough and sometimes unpopular decisions in order to survive.

In an ideal world, most academicians would like to be able to disregard marketplace and economic realities. They would like to design a college that offers what they believe to be the ideal curriculum, typically one that minimizes what classical academicians somewhat condescendingly refer to as vocational training, and which sometimes includes majors in business and education. Rather, they would insist that all undergraduate students pursue a broad-based liberal education in the arts and sciences, which many strongly believe is the best training for a lifetime of learning and growing. And they are not wrong.

The problem is that such an ideal curriculum is not necessarily what paying customers are prepared to buy. *The Chronicle of Higher Education* 2012 Almanac reports that, in 2012, 1.65 million degrees were awarded and nearly 25% were in business and administration. Another 15% were in health professions and education. Engineering degrees and Communications degrees represented another 10%. Visual and performing arts comprised another 5%.

Over half of all college students are not interested in broad-based liberal arts majors, so any college narrowing itself accordingly takes on greater challenges when recruiting students. In fact, only 13% of all college students are liberal arts majors, which grows to 30% if the additional 17% of psychology and sociology students are included. Any college that positions itself as a purely liberal arts college has greatly narrowed its potential student applicant pool.

In that same ideal world, most academicians are repelled by the prospect of denying admission to any academically

promising student who cannot afford to pay tuition.

This is a noble ideology that few would want to oppose. After all, academically qualified and motivated students shouldn't be denied admission to the college of their choice. The richest and most heavily endowed of the 1,700 independent small colleges can enroll a quite large proportion of financially needy students without significant consequence as they have alternative sources of revenue generated from their endowment investments. However, the other 1,500 independent colleges cannot forgo tuition revenue without seriously impairing their financial ability to operate.

The average tuition rate, not counting room, board, books and expenses, for 2012 among independent colleges is $28,500 (*Chronicle of Higher Education* 2012 Almanac). Even those colleges that discount as much as 50% and sometimes higher, still leave financially needy students with having to pay the other half, at least $14,000 annually, along with as much as another $5,000 to $6,000 in additional costs.

The national median family income for 2011 was $51,413, before taxes (2011 US Labor Dept Economic Study reported in *USA Today*, February 9, 2012), meaning *at least HALF* the families in America cannot possibly set aside as much as $20,000 for a child's annual college costs. Yet, at the same time, no college wants to close its door on anyone who cannot afford to attend, but is otherwise academically promising.

This understandable reluctance is nevertheless creating a national phenomenon among small, enrollment-revenue colleges that is becoming known as the Full Enrollment Structural Deficit outcome.

That is, these colleges see themselves as 'successfully' enrolling a full cohort of students while at the same time are not realizing anywhere close to the revenues they need to operate at even the minimal levels of acceptability.

In reality, there isn't an ideal solution. Colleges have to pay employees, most of whom consider themselves underpaid as it is. Colleges are not exempt from electric and oil bills. Equipping classrooms with state-of-the-art technology is expected by all students, regardless of how little they may be paying. The list goes on of obligatory costs that keep growing year after year.

This dilemma has many pundits forecasting the demise of many of the 1,500 heavily enrollment-revenue dependent colleges, especially those that continue to offer academic programs of little interest to the majority of college students and those institutions that, for all intents and purposes, 'sell' the product for less than it costs to make it. No such college can continue to over-enroll students who simply cannot afford to pay the necessary tuition rates. All colleges must face the responsibility that they must realize sufficient revenue to operate at an acceptable level of effectiveness.

Those colleges caught up in this unfortunate reality, and most are, have no choice but to rethink their academic and enrollment ideals, and instead retool in order to attract a larger proportion of the college-bound student pool, and especially (whether they like it or not) those families in the position to pay a tuition rate that at least approximates the actual monies needed to operate.

Over the past several decades, discounting has at least kept pace with, and too often exceeded, tuition increases resulting in, at best, no additional revenues from tuition. Too many colleges have found themselves realizing fewer revenues going forward as their discount rate has been growing at a rate outpacing the actual tuition rate. This trend cannot continue for any institution aspiring to survive, much less flourish.

Possessing the proverbial 'fiduciary responsibility' for their colleges, Trustees must ask questions about their colleges that are (Heaven Forbid) not unlike those they would ask if they were overseeing a business. This approach inevitably appalls many academics, who will likely argue against emulating corporate methodology in any way, contending that higher education must be void of market influences and should not be influenced by financial realities.

To the contrary, colleges and universities should be led by those who insist on maintaining the 'highest standards' of academic resources and somehow find a way to finance the costs. Nice work if you can get it, but in today's real world, the costs of running a college have skyrocketed to a point where most institutions simply can no longer jump off bridges to prove the law of gravity. Someone has to take a lead in confronting the facts and advocating a more viable approach that will call upon many of the 1,500 enrollment-revenue dependent institutions to stop trying to be all things to all people and instead start accepting that they lack the wherewithal to emulate the billion-dollar-endowed research universities. . .and always will.

This is where Boards of Trustees must step up to the plate. Trustees have both the legal and the fiduciary responsibility to insure that the college or university is proceeding responsibly and not digging for itself a hopelessly bottomless pit, aimlessly constructing FULL

11

ENROLLMENT STRUCTURAL DEFICITS that inevitably will drive some institutions to bankruptcy.

Many of the needed tough decisions will likely find little support within the institution, especially among faculty, because they are likely to include reducing the number of academic majors when too few students are being enrolled to support them. Another unpopular decision will be changing the admissions recruiting strategies to enrolling fewer students who cannot afford to attend without receiving discounts that come close to full scholarships.

To be clear, this book is not intended to 'mobilize' Trustees to become more pro-active in the hands-on management of the college they are overseeing.

To the contrary, that is a President's job and the Board should not be doing his/her job.

The Board's role is to be vigilant with respect to the way in which the President and

the senior officers are conducting their responsibilities.

In order to do this well, Trustees must have an reasonable understanding of the nature of higher education administration. In the corporate sector, Boards of Directors are typically appointed from among comparable business leaders. . .people who understand the nature of the business and can ask the kinds of questions that stimulate and challenge senior management.

To the contrary, college Trustees rarely have higher education management experience and are therefore too often overly dependent on their management teams to understand what they do not. As a result, they often defer to management by accepting their views on the state of the institution without asking their own questions based on their personal expertise.

Recently, The Pennsylvania State University Board of Trustees was nationally condemned because, in the view of most, their members did not ask the tough questions often enough and thereby didn't insure that institutional leadership had acted in a timely manner to prevent more serious consequences, not to mention doing what was right.

Too many Boards learn about a disaster only after it is too late to prevent it.

13

Hopefully this book will provide Trustees with a useful checklist of typical oversights so they can read the red flags and act in the very best interests of their institution while there is still time to nip crisis in the bud.

Chapter 2

Higher Education
is changing faster than
some colleges can handle

T O repeat a very important point, this book has been prepared principally for Trustees (and Presidents) of heavily enrollment revenue-dependent, non-public colleges and universities, especially those colleges not enrolling the number of students they need, and, more critically, not enrolling enough paying students to generate the necessary revenues to cover essential operating costs. 'Heavily dependent' defines those colleges and universities where tuition and related enrollment revenues (room, board

15

and fees) comprise more than 90% of annual revenues. Such institutions are also modestly endowed (less than $200 million), with minimal research revenues and virtually no government funding. They are the most vulnerable to the economic and demographic conditions facing independent higher education in the turbulent times that characterize these early years of the 21st century. . .turbulence which isn't likely to subside anytime soon.

The changes that have occurred, and continue to intensify, over the past decade or so since the beginning of the new millennium, are jarring. The most striking changes include the following factoids, as reported in *The New York Times*, on May 12, 2012 *(in the feature "A Generation Hobbled by the Soaring Cost of College" written by Andrew Martin and Andrew W. Lehren)*:

American family wealth has dropped by 40% since 2007, and has returned to the wealth levels of the 1950s.

Nearly half (49%) of all college graduates since 2006 have not found a full-time job.

Nearly one-third of all adults under 30 years old are still living at home because they cannot afford to live on their own.

Over 48% of all college graduates owe more than $10,000 in student loans.

Since 2006, over two million students a year, who previously opted for a college degree, have shifted to vocational training schools to better insure, they believe, that they will find a job upon graduation.

Like it or not, heavily tuition-dependent institutions have to increasingly face up to the realities that any comparable small business must confront. . .most notably that. . .

no product can be sold for an amount that is less than what it costs to make, and, for that matter, no product should exist that virtually no one wants to purchase.

Trustees must bite the bullet and become more aggressive in asking the questions that insure the institution is managing itself realistically. The days of a bottomless pit of revenue are long gone, if, indeed, such times ever really existed. Colleges, especially the heavily enrollment

17

dependent ones, can no longer disregard the reality that they must think like a business to insure future viability and fiscal health.

There was a time when a college education was seen by parents as the road to a better life for their children. Along with housing costs and medical costs, sending children to college was viewed as an absolute necessity regardless of the debt that might be incurred in order to enable that gateway to the future.

As the media has been reporting, the gig is up.

Student debt now exceeds one trillion dollars. . .*that is one million, million dollars*. Student debt is greater than total American credit card debt.

Consider this: Assume the 1,500 tuition-dependent independent colleges and universities in America have an average enrollment of 2,000 students and an average annual operating budget of about $60 million. That makes the total annual expense of running all these colleges about ninety billion dollars. At that annual rate, it would take over 11 years for total expenditures of all private colleges in America to total the one trillion dollars in student debt that has been accumulated by college students.

You heard that right, and it bears repeating . . .
college student debt already accumulated equals over a decade of operating costs of ALL 1,500 enrollment-revenue institutions.

In addition to student debt . . .
debt incurred by American colleges and universities has doubled to over $300 billion in just the past decade.

Colleges simply can't keep expecting to enroll students who can't afford to pay the skyrocketing costs of private higher education. And, colleges can't hope to survive by discounting their tuition, at levels not uncommonly exceeding 50% of tuition rates, in order to seduce financially-strapped families into paying the other 50% that they really don't have and cannot afford. For too many decades, academics have advocated accessibility to expensive private higher education regardless of financial wherewithal. No one should be denied access to the 'college of their choice' because they cannot afford it. Sounds very noble and perhaps it is. But, enrollment-dependent institutions simply cannot afford to enroll too many students who are, in turn, unable to pay the tuition. Yet, the reality remains that tuition is the principal source of all expenses including faculty salaries, which faculty typically want increased while, at the same time, advocating lower tuition rates from the only source funding those sought-after increases.

Costs keep going up every year. Net revenues, unfortunately, seem to be going down every year as fewer students can afford to pay anything close to the tuition rates being charged, and then discounted. The tuition-dependent colleges have to go back to the drawing board and face the reality that they cannot be all things to all people. Trustees have to challenge their institutions when no one else will.

Independent external audits of colleges and universities are not as comprehensive, and certainly not as scrutinizing, as Trustees may be inclined to presume. Yes, there is an annual audit of the operating budget and financial balance sheet. While such audits evaluate bottom line fiscal health, or lack thereof, not much more is assessed including the root causes of looming financial difficulties.

The only other major external audit is academic accreditation assessments, most notably conducted by the regional accrediting bodies. These evaluations occur in depth only once a decade. While they are conducted on-site by a committee of external higher education professionals, usually chaired by a college or university president, their work can be more limited than Trustees might presume, especially with respect to vital signs that can financially make or break an institution.

ONE MILLION DOLLARS
is a 43 inch high stack of $100 bills
ONE BILLION DOLLARS
is nearly THREE Empire State Building-high stacks of $100 bills

ONE TRILLION DOLLARS

...or the present size of outstanding college student debt
which boggles sensibilities no matter how you look at it !!

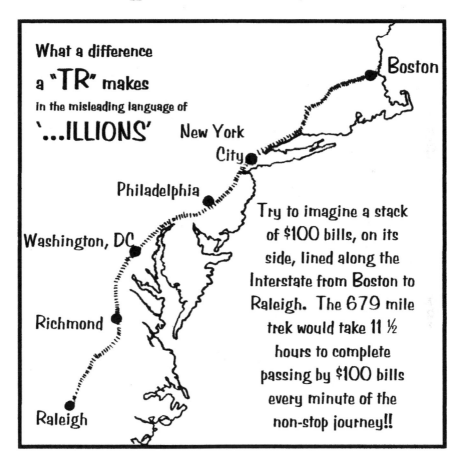

What a difference

a "TR" makes

in the misleading language of

'...ILLIONS'

New York City

Boston

Philadelphia

Washington, DC

Richmond

Raleigh

Try to imagine a stack of $100 bills, on its side, lined along the Interstate from Boston to Raleigh. The 679 mile trek would take 11 ½ hours to complete passing by $100 bills every minute of the non-stop journey!!

or, if that doesn't do it for you, imagine

2,867 Empire State Building stacks of $100 bills

The management of any institution, when reporting to the Board of Trustees, is likely to put as positive a spin as it can fashion on all indicators of institutional performance. Calling the glass half-full, instead of half-empty is an understandable motivation. The same sort of behavior occurs within for-profit organizations when management reports to the Board of Directors and even more so when reporting to stockholders.

Performance indicators can be spun in ways that don't reveal what could be longer term problems in the making. In business, the consequences of such spins can be seen in the collapse of major financial institutions like Lehmann Brothers and more recently, in 2012, with the $6 billion loss at JPMorgan.

A higher education-themed positive spin, for example, might be to report a 10% increase in fund raising, which upon closer examination may have been realized by a much larger increase in spending to achieve that improvement, thereby resulting in a net decline in spendable donations.

Similarly, a heralded uptick in enrollment could really be a loss in actual enrollment

revenues if unfunded grant aid was increased in order to enroll those additional students.

To the contrary, a decrease in total enrollment could actually be an increase in net student revenues if unfunded grant aid were significantly reduced.

Such examples scratch the surface of a collection of questions that Trustees should be asking when presented with management reports of institutional performance. Each chapter of this book will focus on a vital sign that, if not thoroughly scrutinized, could contribute to institutional crisis and financial demise. Trustees who use these signs to ask the right questions may be viewed as annoying busybodies, but in doing so, may prove to be an institutional savior. As goes the old adage:

THE RIGHT DECISION IS NOT ALWAYS POPULAR.

THE POPULAR DECISION IS NOT ALWAYS RIGHT.

Chapter 3

Admissions:
The Institutional Lifeblood

It's the economy, stupid doesn't only apply to
politicians. For the 1,500 or so enrollment revenue
dependent institutions in the US, 'economy' changes
to 'enrollment revenue' and the remainder of the
point is unchanged.

**Nothing else works, or even matters, at an
institution unable to find, enroll _and keep_ paying
customers.** While this vital sign is usually referred to as,
and overseen by, admissions, the word 'admissions' is

somewhat of a misnomer for the work that must be done because 'admissions' conjures up a process where the focus is to assess the qualifications of applicants and select who, from among the presumable masses, merits an invitation to enroll. While this evaluative step is part of the process, it is in fact the least essential part for smaller, tuition-dependent colleges.

Granted that several hundred of the most heavily endowed independent colleges and universities in the US *do* have the luxury of being able to characterize their 'admissions' offices accordingly, because evaluation and selection is largely what they are doing. Harvard, for example, seeks to enroll 1700 new students each year and receives 30,000 applications. Not all that much effort, at Harvard, has to be expended in finding those 30,000 applications. The main task at Harvard's admissions office is selecting the mere 6% of applicants who are admitted. Therefore, in Harvard's relatively rare case, the designation "Admissions" applies.

Needless to say, all colleges and universities would like to be enjoying Harvard's cornucopia of applicants. However, ALL BUT the top hundred or so colleges and universities instead need to think more like the sales and marketing department of a consumer products company. Many don't understand that, and/or don't like the sound of that reality. As a consequence, they fail to deliver 'the economy, stupid' for their institution.

Monitoring the admissions process is not easy. The operational lingo/jargon among college admissions professionals is extensive, making it a challenge for college presidents and trustees to fully assess what is actually going on. The confusion is amplified by the way in which college rating organizations, like *USNews & World Report Best Colleges*, focus on measurements that often don't accurately reflect successful admissions practices, especially economically successful practices.

Rating organizations like *USNews* may well be using statistics at top performing institutions like Harvard as a benchmark for all of higher education. For instance, because Harvard has the luxury of selecting only 1700 admits from among 30,000 applications, their extraordinary 6% 'admit rate' has become the standard used by rating organizations to ascertain the academic excellence of all colleges and universities. That is, academic excellence thereby correlates to being in the position to reject 94%, or at least a large portion, of your applicants.

Conventional wisdom has seemingly evolved in such a way as to establish the tenet that the more applicants who are rejected, the better the academic quality of the student body. This correlation is a specious one, but nevertheless results in many colleges seeking to optimize the size of their applicant pool so they, too, can reject a prerequisite number of their aspiring students. Upon doing so, they can then presumably characterize themselves as 'competitive,' or 'selective,' and thus improve their prospects of being ranked as a higher quality institution.

To get a monitoring handle on the complex process, the important definitions in admissions jargon 'begin at the beginning' with quantifying the number of prospective students, most usually referred to as:

Prospects/Inquiries

The most important part of this group comprises those students who initiate an expression of interest. However, it often includes other students with fewer expressed interests, even including names from lists that can be bought from educational testing services. Eventually, though, this starting group will be whittled down to become the pool of prospective students designated as . . .

Applicants

'Applicants' should be those students who have completed all parts of the application process including having paid an application fee. Some colleges have eliminated fees in order to increase their applicant pool, a factor that should be questioned when massive increases in application rates are cited as a measurement of success. At any rate, applicants are then assessed for their academic qualifications, resulting in some being denied and others forming a group called . . .

Admits

'Admits,' logically enough, are those applicants who are 'notified' that they have been 'selected' and are thereby invited to inform the institution as to whether they will accept the admit offer, by submitting a cash deposit to reserve a seat, thereby comprising the 'yield' from the ADMIT pool typically called . . .

Deposits/Yield on Admits

'Deposits' have traditionally been those students who accepted the admit offer and sent along a financial deposit in order to 'reserve' their place in the incoming class. Some colleges are no longer requiring a deposit and, in doing so, create much greater uncertainty about the student acceptance of the admit offer. Others have greatly reduced the size of the deposit, or have made it refundable should the student change his/her mind. This similarly adds uncertainty to the student commitment to attend. Therefore, admissions offices shouldn't conclude their work is done when the deposit is received (More about this later in the chapter). Hopefully, most 'depositors' will not change their mind and, if not, in the fall of each year, 'deposits' become the new cohort of:

Enrolled/Yield on Deposits

Logically enough, these terms form a pyramid where the largest number will always be the PROSPECTS/ INQUIRIES and the smallest will be the final group of ENROLLED students. At each level moving upward to the peak of enrollments, mistakes can be made that can adversely affect the final outcome.

Here are some vital signs that Trustees and Presidents should be looking for at each phase:

Vital Signs of Inquiries

Admissions offices at under-enrolled colleges are most likely to find themselves scrambling to expand the applicant pool which begins at the beginning. . .with prospects or inquiries. Conventional wisdom advances the notion that more inquiries will generate more applications which will increase admits, and so on up the pyramid. Not necessarily.

The number of 'Inquiries' is the easiest statistic to expand, and is rarely a meaningful, or successful, indicator of student demand for the college or university.

When admissions offices are reporting a surge in inquiries, presidents and trustees should be wary, and inquire as to how that outcome actually happened. Too many of the wrong kinds of inquiries can waste time and money, while crowding the pipeline in ways that make it more difficult to separate the wheat from the chaff and allow proper attention to prospects who *are* likely to enroll.

An example of how inquiry numbers can be readily, but counterproductively, inflated is the 'prospect' list accumulated during college fair visits.

Each year, college fairs are sponsored throughout the country where literally hundreds of colleges and universities set up 'booths' in order to allow high school students and their families to begin their college search without actually having to visit campuses. These fairs can be massive and are often considered to be 'must-attend' events for smaller colleges lacking the brand recognition of top schools.

Alumni can be very vocal in their criticism when they visit a college fair with their high school age sons and daughters and don't see their alma mater represented. Hence, any under-enrolled college not participating faces blame for enrollment shortfalls if they are not represented. As smaller colleges lack the staff in admissions to be everywhere at the same time, many colleges call upon

31

alumni volunteers to staff some of these fairs. Such alumni 'ambassadors' can become overzealous in collecting prospects and, in doing so, contribute to a clogged admissions pipeline (i.e., a data base of prospects who have little to no interest in enrolling).

If you observe high school attendees at these fairs, you most usually see students who are wandering from booth to booth carrying a large shopping bag which, almost like Halloween, is being filled to the top with goodies. . .in this case, brochures and other hand-outs. The colleges attending these fairs want the names and the addresses of the student attendees and will typically aspire to optimize the number of students whom they can get to fill out prospect cards. The more inquiry cards they accumulate, the more the admissions representatives will feel they can return to the office as a success. Some colleges will offer freebies like candy bars, and even 'door prizes,' in exchange for a completed inquiry card, which is typically little more than a post card asking for a name, address, high school and year.

High school students attending a college fair can end up completing dozens, maybe even hundreds, of inquiry cards in exchange for giveaways, or sometimes only to accommodate an aggressive institutional representative. Otherwise, they have little to no interest in many of the colleges where they will now be counted as INQUIRIES or PROSPECTS. Five or six recruiters attending college fairs, not to mention alumni volunteers, can amass tens of thousands of post cards that, for the most part, will never result in meaningful applications.

The cost of processing near-worthless inquiries, often referred to as 'phantom' prospects, can be crippling.

First, staffing is required to manually enter all these postcards into a data base. Then, the real costs begin when all these relatively low-yield prospects start receiving what can be a flood of expensive mailings. The college view book alone can cost as much as $10 per prospect, (hopefully) including postage. Over time, as much as $100 or more. . .*PER INQUIRY!!!*.. can be spent in follow-up mailings sent to phantom prospects who have absolutely no interest in your college except for the long ago consumed candy bar that was obtained at the college fair. Smaller, tuition dependent colleges can't afford this kind of financial waste.

Prospect names can also be purchased. The Educational Testing Service (ETS) sells lists of those students taking college entrance examinations. The lists can be purchased by region, by stated academic interests and by test score. Some admissions offices, upon purchasing such lists, add those students to their prospect headcount. Such a statistical surge, having been purchased, in no way constitutes an improvement in prospective student interest in the college even though such data are sometimes reported as such.

At least one Middle Atlantic institution has gone so far as to admit with congratulations, prospects bought from ETS but who otherwise had never expressed a scintilla of interest in the college. The institution bought the names and addresses of top scoring high school students telling them they were admitted even though they hadn't applied. How many of these students accepted the admit offer is not being reported, but zero is a good guess.

The most encouraging facet of an inquiry pool consists of those students who have contacted the college, with an expression of interest, especially if they were referred by their high school counselor or by others whose opinion they trust, including former high school classmates now enrolled at the college. Establishing what is called 'feeder high schools,' namely institutions that annually send applications from students who ultimately enroll, is among the most effective source of student enrollments. . .just like a business would rightly value repeat business from satisfied customers and their referrals.

Admissions offices have to be careful not to clog their pipeline with too many 'phantom' prospects that take precious time away from

focusing on students who are serious about attending.

Thus, any surge in INQUIRIES should be assessed with a critical eye questioning whether more is better. Too many phantom prospects and applications poured into the pipeline can make it that much more difficult to find the needles in the haystack. . .i.e., those students who will accept the admit offer and actually enroll.

Contrary to the way in which admissions data are frequently reported to Trustees (e.g., applications are up!!!), when it comes to measuring the potential success of enrollment recruiting efforts. . .

QUALITY
(OF THE PROSPECT POOL)
IS MORE IMPORTANT THAN QUANTITY.

Probably the most valuable cohort of inquiries/prospects comprises those students who, with their families, visit the college for tours and Open Houses.

The commitment represented by anyone setting aside what is usually most of a day is a much more powerful indication of interest as compared to having completed a

post card at a college fair. Campus visitors should be
flagged in the INQUIRY pool masses to receive a higher
quality of personal attention throughout the admissions
process.

Perhaps the President of Harvard doesn't need to
attend Campus Visit Days in order to assure an optimum
student enrollment, but every one of the 1500, for which this
book has been written, are not Harvard, never will be
Harvard, and shouldn't be using that University as a
roadmap for enrollment success.

**Trustees should, at least once, experience
the on-campus Open House program** in order to
know how the college is being presented to prospects. At
enrollment-dependent smaller colleges, the President should
attend _all_ Open Houses and, presuming he/she is an
effective and uplifting public speaker, should be prominently
featured on the program.

Also, the most engaging faculty should be
prominently featured at all Open Houses and all faculty
should take turns representing their colleagues at these
events. The faculty, more than any other facet of the
college, represents the product being sold and their presence
and involvement is a plus. Faculty participation also
indicates their commitment to the institution's success,
presuming, of course, that they have been invited.

If the President, the Provost and the senior faculty are not participating in Campus Visit Days, the college is not facing up to the importance of these events for its economic viability. . . or, even, its survival.

Vital Signs of Applications

"Applications are up," is an almost universally presumed declaration of success when announced by a college. While it isn't bad news necessarily, there are applications. . .*and.* . .*there are applications.* Trustees should be asking questions about any surge in applications in order to insure that the trend is the good news that it appears, at first glance, to be.

In recent decades, it has become increasingly less costly and more efficient for high school students to submit applications for admission to colleges. Some colleges have eliminated the application fee altogether in order to optimize the number of applications they receive. Also, services like "The Common Application" have become increasingly popular. The Common Application is a membership of colleges and universities (that has become quite large, nearly 500) all of whom have agreed to accept the same application format. Thus, the applicant need fill out only one set of 'paperwork' and send that same completed application to dozens of admissions offices.

37

An enormous incentive exists among admissions office professionals, and sometimes even more senior college officers including the President, to optimize the number of applications received each year. As explained earlier, large applicant pools are often portrayed as a measure of institutional quality. Because of the way in which applicant pool size is viewed, college presidents are too frequently asked about admissions performance as a way of ascertaining how the college is performing. Being able to report 'applications are up' and, as a result, fewer students are winning admission, is among the most desirable responses to such inquiries, thereby demonstrating the college's success, or so conventional wisdom would have you conclude.

However, as with phantom inquiries that can clog the works, phantom applications can be just as counterproductive, if not damaging, to the final outcome.

As many colleges have learned the hard way, apparent floods of applications don't necessarily guarantee a successful enrollment outcome. . .especially if the massive number of applications results in admitting the wrong students and denying, or otherwise disregarding, the right ones; the right ones being those students who will accept the admit offer and actually enroll.

Unless the admissions office is very carefully separating the proverbial wheat from the chaff throughout the inquiry and application process, **the applicant pool could be overcrowded with students who are not very interested in actually attending.**

Particularly fatal is when too many of the most desirable applicants are also those least likely to attend because their first choices are elsewhere. Their status as 'most desirable' can have the admissions office spending too much time and money courting applicants who offer the least likelihood of ever enrolling.

College bound high school students today, especially those contemplating the more expensive independent colleges for whom this book has been written, are typically inclined to submit applications to at least a half dozen colleges and often many more. Anyone applying to Harvard, for instance, stands a 94% chance, from one perspective, of being rejected. So, most students need to apply to "fall back" institutions on which they can rely if all else fails them.

Even major league institutions have had the rug pulled out from under them as a result of badly handling the large applicant pools that they created.

A number of years back, a major national university in the East, designated University X herein, was experiencing impressive application pools each year which permitted a high degree of selectivity. After selecting the 'best and the brightest' from among their applicants, they waited for their 'admits' to 'deposit.' *Virtually none deposited.* All their first-choices had been admitted to Harvard, Yale, Princeton and other gold standard universities which the applicants had ranked as *their* first choice institutions. As a fall-back institution for all their first-round admits, University X was left having to go to their waiting list for nearly the entire freshman class. Because wait-listees had been denied admission in the first wave, many of the better quality wait-listed students opted instead for another institution that wanted them the first time around. This happened year after year until University X finally refocused on those applicants who indicated that University X was their first choice. While many of these students were not academically the very best among the applicant pool, they were very good students and excelled at the university.

Another major urban university in the Middle Atlantic region, which will be named University Y, aggressively sought to grow its enrollments and boasted a more than doubling of its applicant pool which it cited prominently as a demonstration of its successful renaissance. Upon closer examination of its admissions statistics, University Y, like University X, was being viewed as a fall-back choice for most of its preferred applicants. Over 80% of its 'admits' opted to enroll elsewhere, leaving University Y with having to enroll half its freshman class from among its rejects who had been wait listed in the first round of admit decisions.

While this still permitted the University to boast that its freshman class had doubled, it was experiencing a 500 freshman attrition rate . . . students who either dropped out because they were indeed inadmissible (i.e., they shouldn't have been wait listed; they should have been denied), or transferred elsewhere because too many academically unremarkable students were part of its class.

Smaller colleges shouldn't be chasing after surges in applications in order to report progress or success when the result is at the expense of clogging their pipeline with students who are not that attracted to them. Instead they should focus their efforts on quality instead of quantity.

Admissions officers have to know their applicants and be able to identify those students most likely to consider the college to be their first choice. Waiting lists are going to be that much less effective at colleges without national brand name recognition. Therefore, admitting the wrong students and rejecting the right students can result in turning what could have been a successful fall enrollment into a disaster.

Vital Signs of 'Admits'

During what is usually the winter Board of Trustees meeting, operating budgets for the next academic year are presented based largely, in the case of enrollment-revenue dependent colleges, on enrollment projections. At that same time, the admissions office is only able to report the size of the applicant pool and the resulting size of the ADMIT pool.

There is a tendency for Admissions Offices to see their job has being largely completed once they have evaluated all the applications received and notified the lucky students whom they have admitted.

To the contrary, at smaller, tuition-dependent colleges, **the admissions job has just begun when the 'admit' pool has been determined. Likely revenue is dependent on YIELD and that outcome is not assured by the size of the ADMIT pool.**

While Harvard may have the luxury of knowing they will yield 9 of every 10 students they admit, most smaller, tuition-dependent colleges are probably going to be lucky to 'yield' 3 of every 10 students admitted. Typically, a minimum of 1500 students need to be admitted in order to realize 500 freshmen. If the applicant pool has been surging, past yields may not be indicators of future outcomes, thereby making forecasts that much more uncertain.

Trustees should be asking questions, at this point in the admissions process, that reveal how well the admissions staff know the 'admits.'

Some 'admits' can more certainly be projected as likely enrollees. Athletic coaches, for instance, tend to have a very good sense of their new freshmen and their likelihood to commit/enroll. The same is true for other specialized students including those in theater and music programs. Like coaches, professors in these boutique academic programs tend to be very involved in admissions recruiting.

The most uncertain YIELD among 'admits,' unless otherwise verified by admissions officers who know the students well, are at either end of the applicant continuum.

At one end of the continuum are students with very high financial need which includes a contingent of students who are also very academically accomplished. Such students have probably applied to as many schools as they can afford (given application fees) and will likely select whatever college has offered the largest financial aid package . . .because they really have no other choice.

If the 'admit' pool ends up heavily populated with high financial need students, the yield could be much lower than the 30%-35% that is most typical among smaller, tuition-dependent schools. High need students are least likely to be able to afford to enroll even when they receive scholarships that underwrite 50% or more of their costs. Too often, the other 50% that they must pay is beyond their wherewithal. These students are often in search of a full scholarship which no enrollment dependent college can really afford to offer regardless of a student's merit.

At the other end of the continuum are talented academic achievers who do not have high financial need, but expect scholarship offers because of their high grades. These students have also typically applied to an unusually large number of colleges in the hope that one will offer an extraordinary academic scholarship. Their selection, as with high need students, will likely be based on which college offers the most financial aid/scholarship even if the institution is not the one they would most like to attend.

Any admit pool heavily dependent on the extreme ends of such a continuum of applicants will likely experience a lower yield of 'deposits' than forecasted and budgeted.

Vital Signs of 'Deposited Students'

The most telling milestone in the enrollment cycle is the receipt of deposits.

The deposit deadline is usually May 1st at most colleges and universities, thereby marking the moment when students finally decide among what can often be a dozen colleges to which they have applied and have been admitted. As the deposit is money, students presumably are making a reasonably firm commitment. But, not always.

Many colleges no longer require a non-refundable deposit. Others require a relatively small deposit that some students will pay to more than one of the colleges to which they have been accepted, thereby delaying their final decision.

Colleges with small and/or refundable deposits cannot be certain that any of their deposits will actually enroll.

Students have also learned that many colleges that did not receive the deposits they had forecast, start frantically calling their un-deposited admits, offering them additional scholarship money in order to shift their loyalties away from the college where they did choose to deposit.

45

From a Trustee perspective, operating budgets for the coming year should remain very tentative until 'deposits' can be confirmed, at least by payment of non-refundable fees, unless the college has had years of consistent enrollment outcomes that haven't changed in any meaningful way. Due to this phenomenon, some colleges have shifted their fiscal year to the beginning of September, instead of July, so that no spending for the academic year commences until after the fall tuition deadline, which is usually in August.

Vital Signs of 'Enrolled' students

At the fall meeting of the Board of Trustees, the admissions office will typically submit a report profiling the characteristics of the new freshman class. Data like male:female ratio, resident:commuter ratio, average SAT test scores, ethnicity, nationality, home state and other such 'interesting' factoids will typically dominate the outcomes report.

Trustees often hear little about outcomes by source of application.

For instance, how many students who finally enrolled were first introduced to the process via a college fair post card? How many from high school counselor referrals? How many attended an Open House before applying? How many

46

were recruited by coaches or by faculty for boutique academic programs?

How many new students are receiving a need-based grant significantly larger than the average grant aid package? Such high need students may not have the financial wherewithal to afford to attend beyond the first year.

This is a particularly important statistic for tuition-dependent institutions because it can signal a runaway program that, each year going forward, worsens. That is, if most of the students who are actually enrolling are coming from those students with the highest financial need who have been offered the highest discounts, the college is backing itself into a corner of yielding less net revenue because these higher discounts project forward into the next three years.

Tuition-dependent institutions have to keep their eyes on 'yielding' paying customers because they are the ones that are subsidizing the high need students. If the paying students diminish year after year, the college won't be able to afford to maintain the higher discount rates for the students who are opting to attend.

So, it is absolutely necessary that Trustees understand. . .

How many enrolled students are receiving a larger-than-average academic scholarship?

What proportion of athletes were also high-need scholarship recipients?

Too many athletes could indicate that the athletic department, especially in NCAA Division II and III, is using such scholarships as a recruiting magnet.

How many admits, if any, scored below the national average SAT? If any, student retention could be a problem going forward.

Since 60% to 70%, or more, of the admitted students are likely to have declined the admit offer, the admissions office should also be pushed to compare the source demographics of the students who declined the admit offer to the source demographics of those who accepted the admit offer.

If, for instance, virtually all of the college fair inquiries who became applicants subsequently declined the admit offer, perhaps the monies and personnel time spent on college fairs should be redirected to source applicants that produce higher yields.

If most B students who were admitted, and not offered any grant aid, were a significant portion of those students who declined the admit offer, perhaps grant aid is being too heavily allocated to the wrong students and should be more thinly distributed across the board.

Put simply. . . *(and it easier to say than to do):*

Enrollment-revenue dependent institutions will succeed only when they accurately locate, and sustain, an applicant pool of prospective students who rank the college as their top-choice institution and who also have the financial wherewithal to pay a significant portion of the four-year tuition bill.

To the contrary, too many enrollment-revenue dependent institutions employ a shot-gun approach to recruiting, seeking to optimize the number of applications they can amass. Their best prospects then get lost in the crowd and this prevents the admissions staff from properly cultivating them in a way that would optimize the probability of such students accepting the admit offer and ultimately enrolling. In other words, if the applicant pool and admit pool had been smaller with a higher proportion of students citing the institution as 'first choice,' the staff would have been better able to give their prime applicants the kind of attention needed to have those students remain committed to actually enrolling.

Colleges are succeeding when their first-year students typically declare that the institution was their first choice, and not because it offered them the largest scholarship.

Colleges are not succeeding, obviously, when too many of their admitted students decline the admit offer and go elsewhere.

When colleges are not enrolling the students they financially need, they have probably, from the get-go, been pursuing the wrong students. Sometimes, this failure is because the college is aiming too high, perhaps because the faculty is insisting upon a quality of student who just isn't very likely to enroll unless offered a full scholarship.

Enrollment-revenue dependent colleges not ranked in the top one hundred or so of the best colleges and universities in the country shouldn't be chasing after high school valedictorians, especially such students who come from extremely low income backgrounds. Such students are almost destined to be offered a full scholarship somewhere that enrollment-revenue colleges simply can't afford counter-offer.

Properly organized and focused, a college admissions office can build a substantial network of feeder high schools located in areas where families have the kind of financial wherewithal to afford $30,000 to $40,000 a year in tuition, room and board. If they also don't over-populate the applicant pipeline, the admissions staff can focus their attention on students most likely to accept the admit offer thereby increasing the probability that admitted students will enroll.

Any college yielding under 20% of their admits is recruiting the wrong students from the get-go. With 8 out of 10 admits going elsewhere, something is clearly wrong.

Similarly, if too many students declare they enrolled because they opted for the highest scholarship, too many of those same students will not likely stay for four years because the debt they will be incurring, combined with unforeseen costs of attending, will exhaust their families' financial wherewithal to sustain four years.

All these harsh realities don't sit well with many academics who passionately want to realize what they call 'need blind' accessibility to all private colleges and universities.

Actually, enrolling a flourishing class of B students who, for the most part, are able to pay 60% or more of the advertised tuition-room-and-board rates isn't all that bad. B students are good students who can more than fulfill the expectations of most college faculty. And, if they are also paying tuition, faculty need not fear whether their paycheck will be cashable. All in all, most everyone can enjoy a very productive existence if they can learn to live in a world that isn't absolutely perfect.

Of course, no one really wants to prevent talented students from attending the college of their choice because they come from an economic background that prevents them from paying private college tuition.

At the same time, though, **no tuition-dependent college can afford any more, and perhaps never could, to recruit and enroll too many talented students who cannot pay the tuition level that is necessary to cover the operating costs of the college.**

Chapter 4

Financial Aid & Discounting:

Avoiding
Full Enrollment Structural Deficits

F inancial aid, most notably what is typically called unfunded grant aid, is both the most important item in need of attention by Presidents and Trustees, and the most controversial, misunderstood and hazardous facet of college enrollment management.

Handled badly, which is often the case, a failed grant aid strategy can generate enrollment growth while at the same time causing an ultimately bankrupting enrollment revenue decline. Unfunded grant aid (meaning no revenue source from which the grant is paid) is synonymous with discounting, and discounting is synonymous with foregoing income. Such grant aid is not coming from the government and is not being funded by scholarship endowments or any other gift. Rather, the granting institution is simply doing without the tuition and fees it is otherwise claiming to charge and, too often, the basis (or phantom source) for operating budget expenses that had been Board-approved on the assumption that enrollments would generate revenues to cover those expenses.

In business, such a practice would be construed as increasing market share by reducing the price. Doing so might double the actual sales, but if the price was reduced by 50%, there would be, at best, no improvement to net revenues or, worse, a loss of net revenues. In many cases, excessive product discounting has led some companies to the point where they are selling the product for less than what it is costing to make and market.

There is more than one story of a major retailer that went bankrupt in its quest to increase volume by reducing prices. The more they sold, the more they lost until, finally, they closed down. Too many tuition-dependent colleges are ominously following in a similar potentially fatal path by annually enrolling new student classes at higher and higher discount rates, viewing such a strategy as the only way in which they can enroll their targeted number of students.

Such enrollment growth 'strategies' permit the institution to herald full enrollments, an outcome which is conveyed far and wide as a great success. To the contrary, such outcomes are becoming widely characterized as FULL ENROLLMENT STRUCTURAL DEFICITS, and, as such, the antithesis of strategic success.

When colleges report their enrollments, they usually cite FULL-TIME EQUIVALENT (FTE) students. One FTE is a student taking a full course load each semester which, for traditional four-year, largely residential colleges comprises most of the student body. Where a typical course load is, say, four courses per semester, one annual FTE would be a student taking eight or more courses per academic year. When citing FTE's, the revenue expectation directly correlates to the tuition rate being charged for a full-time student.

If, however, a college has a substantial part-time student contingent (commuting evening students, for example), eight students, each taking one course per academic year, would equal one FTE. Thus, it is possible for some institutions to have half as many FTE's as their 'headcount.'

Trustees and presidents need to closely monitor NET FTE's . . . with the emphasis on NET.

As any tuition-dependent college trustee or president knows, financial aid has skyrocketed in the past several decades to the point where it is no longer unusual for many such colleges to be discounting their tuition, on average, by as much as 50% or much more. Any scholarship offered to any student, whether for reasons of financial need, academic merit or other rationale, like athletics, is in reality a loss of revenue.

When a college of, say, 2,000 FTE's is, on average, discounting tuition by 50% because of unfunded scholarships granted to students, it in fact has a NET FTE of only 1,000 students. **Half of their FTE count is paying nothing and contributing zero to the operating costs of the institution.**

When 1,000 net equivalent students are paying nothing, these same students are adding substantially to the operating cost of the institution. One thousand students are not accommodating a few otherwise empty seats at the back of the classroom. Rather, they are forcing the addition of classes taught by faculty that have to be hired. . .and paid. Furthermore, the cost of housing and feeding full need students (who pay little or nothing) can be substantial, especially in terms of utilities and food costs that would otherwise not be incurred.

The cost of all those free FTE's at enrollment dependent institutions is being accommodated by the other half of the NET FTE who are paying to attend and who are therefore underwriting the 1,000 free FTE's, often by incurring crippling debt.

Some view this phenomenon as a redistribution of wealth in order to provide accessibility for the poor. However, most of the 'payers' are not as wealthy as many seem to presume, and as the trillion dollar student debt hauntingly refutes.

At many colleges, enrollment growth, and even enrollment stabilization, is too frequently reported only in terms of headcount and FTE, with no reference to NET outcomes. **Net enrollment declines have occurred at many tuition-dependent colleges that have at the same time been reporting, and even boasting, enrollment increases.**

Think of it this way: 1,000 students receiving an average discount of 30% reduces the net student enrollment to 700. If the total student FTE grows to 1,200 students while, concurrently, the average discount inflates to 50%, the NET student enrollment has actually dropped 100 students to 600, not increased 200 students to 1,200. So, it is possible for a college to boast an enrollment increase of 200 students while actually experiencing a drop of 100 students. Some colleges boast being full to capacity while, from a fiscal perspective, being anything but.

Ironically, such a self-congratulating college has added to its costs while concurrently generating less revenue. What they are portraying as a success story is actually a failure. Increasingly this phenomenon is being characterized as sometimes fatally "achieving" a "full enrollment structural deficit."

There is no getting away from the reality, sad to say, that tuition-dependent independent colleges have to focus a meaningful component of their recruiting strategies and their financial aid policies on finding and enrolling _mostly_ paying customers.

To that end, college admissions recruiting efforts, and financial aid/discounting policy, have to be tied to outcomes that deliver adequate numbers of students who are willing and able to pay a substantial portion of the tuition being charged. This reality rubs a lot of higher education folks the wrong way as we all would like a world where no one is prevented from attending the college of their choice because of their inability to pay. While such revenue-blind concepts are noble ideals that no one would want to oppose, ideologically, tuition-dependent colleges, by definition, cannot survive if they adopt such unrealistic operating principles. Too many small colleges are headed toward financial demise because they are without a realistic answer as to how they are going to be able to pay their bills when too many of their students are not paying tuition.

In the past few years, a group of college presidents have been leading a campaign calling upon all college presidents to commit themselves to allocating all grant aid, unfunded or otherwise, singularly on the basis of financial need. These same presidents have expressed alarm at trends where colleges are allocating their grants based on merit, including athletic talent. In doing so, students with lesser financial need receive grants they arguably don't need, but become incentives for them to enroll.

The advocates for an all-need-based grant philosophy further point to declines in low-income and minority students at those colleges redirecting their grant aid to merit. At national meetings, including the Presidents' Institute of the Council of Independent Colleges, these presidents have presented a set of principles which they are calling upon all college presidents to adopt which include:

-striving, as a matter of policy, to meet full need.

-giving priority to meeting full need.

-eliminating the concept of 'merit,' since all aid
     recipients should be considered meritorious.

The pressure seems to be growing, including in media accounts and, reportedly among government officials, for all college presidents to adopt these need-only grant aid principles which could well be an impossible dream that could lead to fatal financial consequences if not carefully monitored. . .and, even IF carefully monitored.

Meeting the full need of all admissible students could lead many colleges to the point where virtually all of their students have a need level that makes them eligible for close to full scholarships. **Tuition dependent colleges cannot afford to take their eye off the recruitment of students whose families can afford to pay.**

The presidents advocating need-only financial aid are hoping, presumably, that incentives other than money can persuade paying students to opt for their college instead of one of the other five or six colleges to which that student has also been admitted. If all colleges abandoned all forms of grant aid except need, perhaps college choice would indeed no longer be influenced by grant aid inducements.

Revenue dependent colleges, though, can't really afford to take such a risk unless they are certain they can successfully recruit and enroll students who can afford to pay.

Tuition dependent colleges also have to limit the amount of financial need they meet. **No tuition-dependent college can meet ALL student need that comes its way.**

When a college offers a financially needy student less than what constitutes full need, too often that needy student enrolls anyway and incurs debt that exceeds an amount that they can realistically be expected to pay back. By the end of their sophomore or junior year, such students are hopelessly in debt as are the institutions that have enrolled more non-paying students than they can afford. As such, a well-intended institution is arguably disserving needy students by luring them to enroll, taking as much money as they can get, and thereby inducing well-intended students into incurring debt they will likely be unable to repay, knowing that these same students will be over-indebted long before they graduate and will be forced to drop out for financial reasons.

No college can claim to be advocating equal access when they admit needy students they cannot financially support throughout their undergraduate experience. Such well-intended institutions are creating more of a problem than they are solving as they are luring students who cannot afford a four-year tenure unless fully subsidized, which no enrollment-revenue dependent college can possibly afford to underwrite for any significant portion of their student body.

Vital Signs of Unfunded Grant Aid/Discounts

Trustees need to be asking questions about the way in which unfunded grant aid is allocated and how that affects the yield of admits. . .i.e., those who deposit and enroll.

Note that discounts are offered to applicants when they are admitted and long before they have accepted that admit offer. Most colleges feel they are succeeding when less than two-thirds of those students admitted decline the offer and go elsewhere. So, for every ten students admitted, and offered a discount, only three or four (sometimes fewer) of those ten students will enroll.

This is where it gets complicated. For every ten students admitted, some are offered as much as a total scholarship, some are offered no discount at all, and others are offered an amount somewhere between nothing and everything. If all ten students were to accept the admit offer, the average discount rate may well result in a financially manageable ratio of, say, 35% of gross revenues.

But, what if all the applicants who were offered no discount decline the admit offer and go elsewhere? And, what if the only two students who accept the admit offer were the ones granted full scholarships? The average discount rate that was supposed to come in at 35% has instead turned out to be a crippling 100%. . .meaning that no income whatsoever has been realized from the admit pool. Needless to say, this is an extreme worst-possible-case outcome, but it does illustrate that when, on average, 7 out of 10 admits don't enroll, it is almost impossible to forecast, in advance, who will actually enroll.

On the other hand, it is relatively logical to presume that there will be a particularly strong correlation between those students offered the highest discounts, and those students who are among the small percentage of 'admits' who accept their admit offer and enroll.

If 500 new students are sought, and the yield is less than 20% of those admitted, over 2,500 must be admitted in order to yield 500 who actually enroll. How is it possible to know which students will be among that one-third who deposit? What if the 500 who deposit are all admits who have been offered the highest levels of unfunded grant aid? If that happens, the college could end up having sold the product, so to speak, for far less than it will cost to make it.

The only way in which any kind of yield prediction is possible is to meticulously study outcomes over the period of several years in order to be able to identify consistent trends. This requires a very thorough understanding of the characteristics of the students who have been admitted and an equally consistent financial aid strategy, neither of which is likely to be in place at those institutions with runaway discount rates.

A frequent mistake is allocating most of the discounts to the highest financial need students and to top academic achievers.

Of particular concern to the financial well being of any tuition-dependent college is enrolling too many students who finally just cannot afford to pay their share of the tuition bill. If a college's annual tuition, room and board costs exceed, say, $30,000, which is not uncommon, then even a 50% scholarship requires the student to find the other $15,000 from personal resources and loans. Over a four year college span, that is $60,000 (not counting personal expenses, books, etc) which is far more than virtually any high need student can possibly afford.

Too many of these students, having been offered a 50% or more 'scholarship,' will stretch themselves to their financial limit in the first year and dig a hole for themselves that makes it impossible for them to stay enrolled without additional institutional discounts that the college cannot afford to offer no matter how accomplished the student proves to be. The student, to the contrary, hopes the college will want to keep them and will be more generous over the four year span.

Not infrequently, faculty become involved appealing to the administration to keep an exceptional student. By accommodating such appeals, **the NET enrollment revenue can decline even more over the four year span of a student class overpopulated with high discounted students.**

Many companies that specialize in financial aid consulting have found that the highest yields among admitted students can come from those who are neither the highest academic achievers, nor the most in financial need. The so-called 'B' student from middle-income families often tends to get ignored when allocating limited grant aid. They are not academically distinguished enough for the scholarships aimed at grade performance, and they are not financially needy enough for the grant aid set aside for low income. Yet, these middle-of-the-continuum students are often the most likely to choose the institution as their first preference. Allocating some scholarships to this large group of admits could greatly improve yield while keeping the average grant aid discount lower than would otherwise be the case.

Yet, this strategy, as previously reported, is now being condemned by a growing contingent of college presidents, and their professional associations, and the media, and government agencies which at the same time seem to be calling for all colleges, regardless of their dependence on enrollment revenue, to meet the full need of all academically qualified students who wish to attend.

How this will play out remains to be seen, but while meeting the "full need" of all students may sound noble and responsible, most tuition-dependent colleges simply cannot afford such a sweeping financial commitment.

Chapter 5

Full-need Grant Aid

An Impossible Dream?

C alling upon all college presidents to implement an exclusively 'need-based' financial aid policy, and a full need commitment to boot, is but the latest overture in what has been repeated attempts to disregard the reality that most independent colleges are heavily enrollment revenue dependent and therefore cannot be what they would ideally like to be. The annual costs of running a small college are very high, especially in the traditional configuration that features expansive acreage and physical plant (sometimes more than needed) along with an attempt to offer every academic major in existence. Somebody has to pay for all that and too many college professors, provosts and presidents don't think it should be students and their families. No student should pay any more than he/she can afford which means that something like 95% of all college students, maybe more, can't afford to pay what colleges need if they are truly going to offer everything they are promising at a level of quality that students and their families expect.

To call upon all college presidents to meet the financial need of all qualified students who apply is tantamount to calling upon the college to turn its back on fiscal reality in order to achieve a romantic ideal of accessibility for all.

While distasteful to what appears to be a growing number of higher education leaders, small colleges have no choice but to recruit a critical mass of students who have the wherewithal to pay a substantial portion, if not all, of the tuition and fees being charged. Students who have that financial wherewithal also have the institutional pick of the litter, assuming they have reasonably good academic records. The factors influencing final college choice among these students are varied and, in many cases, are directly impacted by a financial incentive.

While it may sound inappropriate to offer a scholarship to secure a good student from a financially comfortable family, not doing so could result in financial disaster for many small colleges if they dispense all of their financial aid to high need students. These colleges also have to face the reality that most high need students can't afford to pay tuition PERIOD. Even 80% scholarships require students to come up with $6,000-$10,000 of additional monies not to mention their living expenses, textbooks and supplies.

No enrollment revenue college has much of a chance of survival if they cannot successfully enroll paying customers and a financial aid policy that disregards this reality is tantamount to financial suicide.

The educational leaders advocating a need-only grant aid policy should consider what has been going on for decades since the massive public university build-up during the 1960's post-WWII baby boom. Prior to this public university expansion, two-thirds of all college students attended independent colleges and universities. Today, that ratio is reversed.

Throughout this evolution, lawmakers were citing the public universities as the solution to accessibility for the poor. In New York State, for instance, a vast network of state universities (SUNY) and city universities (CUNY) were portrayed as a Godsend for the poor. It was not been uncommon to hear political leaders declare, 'If if weren't for

SUNY and CUNY, only the rich would get a college education.'

To the contrary, the network of over 100 independent universities and colleges throughout New York State consistently cite a higher graduation rate of minority and low income students.

Equally interesting and important for enrollment-revenue colleges to realize, however, is that the majority of students enrolled in state universities throughout New York, and, for that matter elsewhere, come from families who are not low income. In fact, many come from the highest income families, ones that can afford to pay full tuition at the independent college of their choice.

For 2012-13, SUNY tuition and fees are about $6,900 per year. By comparison, the average independent college annual tuition fees are $28,500. That is quite a difference and enough for many financially-comfortable, and even affluent, families to think twice about the value of an independent college degree, especially if they are being offered no scholarship of any kind as now being proposed by many college presidents.

Curiously, SUNY and CUNY, while citing accessibility for the needy, charge the same low tuition rate regardless of financial wherewithal.

A $6,900 annual tuition rate is a $21,000 scholarship granted to all students, even those whose parents are billionaires.

Affluent parents have long been cited as having pondered this four-year, $80,000+ savings with their college bound children with an offer like . . . *'We can send you anywhere you want to go, but, if you opt for SUNY, you can buy that BMW you have wanted and we will still have money left over.'* The student parking lots of state universities show how that offer all too frequently turns out.

After two years at SUNY, some of those BMW drivers have been known to transfer to what had been their private college of choice, thereby saving $40,000 and earning the same degree, in the same time, as those students who spent four years at the private college.

While tuition-dependent colleges can't hope to survive if they try to compete head-on with state universities, they can't swing to the opposite extreme and decline to use pricing as an incentive in college decision making. Especially daunting is that state universities continue to offer $20,000 annual subsidies without regard to financial need, as they have been doing for decades without being challenged by those who are now calling upon financially-struggling, tuition-dependent colleges to focus their efforts on enrolling students who cannot afford to pay.

73

Trustees have to insist that higher education leaders focus on the financial realities of being an enrollment-dependent institution and thereby decline to march into financial oblivion in order to pursue a 'noble cause' that is, in reality, a fiscal Armageddon.

Trustees should be fully apprised of the distinctive financial aid programs in their particular state and how they specifically affect tuition-dependent institutions. If lawmakers truly supported the tenet that all students, regardless of financial need, should have access to the college or university of their choice, they would establish a grant aid funding system that turned the grant aid over to the student, allowing the student to use that money at any accredited college or university, public or private.

Such a concept works well for food and probably should have been instituted for education from the start. Governments never chose to establish public-owned and managed supermarkets where the poor had to shop. In all likelihood, such markets, had they been established, wouldn't compare qualitatively to the private supermarkets and would be condemned by those who were forced to use them.

Rather, all eligible needy families are given some form of script that is the same as cash and can be used at any market they wish to frequent. Why wasn't the same system established for college-bound students if free access to college of choice without consideration of need was essential?

Now that the massive public higher education systems are in place, there is no eliminating them. But, if so many higher education leaders feel so strongly about access that they are calling upon enrollment-revenue dependent colleges to forego revenue in order to meet the full need of all aspiring applicants for admission, the least lawmakers could do is implement similar need-based considerations for students attending public universities.

Chapter 6

Employee Tuition Remission

S peaking of tuition discounting, most college trustees probably have no idea how much cost is being incurred by their college's program of offering free tuition to the dependents of all employees. That number is typically buried in the total cost of tuition discounts and thereby contributes to what in many cases is a runaway problem of foregone enrollment revenue.

While such a program, once implemented, is almost impossible to take back, Trustees should at least know what the college has gotten itself into and, perhaps over time, can correct.

Employee tuition remission is perhaps one of the most generous compensation benefits in existence anywhere.

Remarkably, the federal government has elected to disregard any taxability of the benefit which today represents a $30,000 to $40,000 pay supplement in after-tax dollars. As all other families must pay college tuition from taxed dollars, the real benefit for each tuition-free dependent can be in excess of $50,000 per year, which in many cases, exceeds the base salary of the employee.

Sometimes, the benefit gets even better as many colleges have placed no limit on the number of dependents eligible for free rides. While not as common, it is not inconceivable that an employed parent could enroll several children at the same time. Three full tuitions could have an employed secretary or mail room clerk making more than the highest paid professors.

Some schools become very dependent, to their financial detriment, on recruiting low-paid staff from the ranks of parents. The misperception has been that such a program doesn't cost the college anything because these students probably wouldn't otherwise enroll and they are just filling proverbially empty

77

seats at the back of the classroom. To the contrary, colleges with dozens of tuition-free dependents of employees have created a situation that can cause significant additional cost that can include hiring more faculty and opening additional courses. Employee children are not limited to enrolling only in courses that are not otherwise fully subscribed. They have full access with the same prerogatives as those students who are paying full tuition.

In some cases, the tuition benefit has been shown to be less than ideal from the perspective of employee stability. Some parents take a college job for only as long as their child is enrolled. Some take jobs they wouldn't otherwise consider in light of the massive equivalent salary being realized. Needless to say, other employees are dedicated, life-long members of the college community, but most institutions don't, and arguably cannot, distinguish between the two.

Speaking of quality, Trustees might also want to inquire as to whether employee dependents must qualify, academically, for admission. Some colleges have allowed dependent tuition remission to become a contractual entitlement that restricts the admissions office from reviewing the academic performance of the dependent. Thus, students with extremely poor high school records are enrolled without paying a cent of tuition, while, conceivably, better students who would have paid full tuition are denied admission.

Colleges with a critical mass of employee dependents in their student body should also be looking at their participation in auxiliary programs like study abroad. One small college that had its own student abroad location in Europe discovered that over half of the students opting for a semester abroad were employee dependents who were therefore contributing nothing to the cost of running the study abroad program. Those who were paying covered less than half the cost of running the program, thereby requiring the college to send cash dollars overseas to support a program that was costing over twice what it was realizing in revenues.

One strategy employed by a college with a high incidence of staff tuition remission for their children was to limit the eligibility among new hires.

Employee dependents became eligible for tuition remission on a graduated basis after the first year of full time employment. In the second year of employment, the remission level was 25%. In the third year, 50%. Only those employees with five years of service received a full tuition remission benefit and only for one dependent at a time.

Each institution is affected to a different degree by the cost of employee tuition remission, some more severely than others. In most cases, Trustees don't know how much revenue is being foregone by this benefit, and, therefore, how much it is contributing to increased costs that are not supported by income. As such, the question should at least be posed so the problem, if there is one, can be understood and hopefully controlled.

Chapter 7

The International Student "Solution?" --- maybe not!

D oes there exist a small, tuition-dependent college anywhere in America that hasn't been advised, at least once, to look into the massive international student market as a way to find full-paying students?

Probably not.

At first glance, the international marketplace does indeed appear to be very promising, if not a limitless cornucopia. Many of the top-ranked universities in America report that they have more international student applications than they can accommodate. The global reputation of American higher education is as good as it could be, representing the international gold standard that places a US university degree as one of the most desirable American products 'made' today.

The Asian-Pacific Belt region of the world is rapidly moving toward accounting for two-thirds of the world's population with China exceeding 1.3 billion and India over 1.2 billion. Together, their 2.5 billion headcount exceeds the USA's mere 310 million by twelve times. No argument that there exist hundreds of millions of young international students from those two countries alone who would love to attend an American university.   And there are tens of millions more from Eastern Europe, Africa and, for that matter, even Western Europe and South America who would also enroll in an American university in a heartbeat.

The Catch-22, though, is that virtually all of these aspiring students can't even afford the air fare to the USA, much less the tuition, room, board and expenses. Sometimes through organizations like the National Association of Foreign Student Advisors (NAFSA), many admissions marketing companies sponsor large college fairs in heavily populated countries like India and China, inviting colleges throughout America to attend and talk to 'tens of thousands' of prospective students. Any college choosing to take the bait and fly one of their admissions counselors to, say, New Delhi will undoubtedly find themselves swamped by students pleading to be admitted. . .but, of course, with the assumption that they will receive a full scholarship including airplane ticket.

From a cultural diversity and enrichment perspective, any college can fill its empty seats with an array of international students that will arguably be a plus to the enrollment experience for all students attending. But, if those international students are being recruited to help improve enrollment revenues, the likelihood is extremely low that such an outcome will be realized. If anything, recruiting and enrolling such students will add expense, not only in admissions travel budgets, but also in student support services.

Are there not any international paying customers that can be found, you ask? As most non-American university students don't comprehend the expectation that they must pay tuition to attend a private university, **international customers prepared to pay tuition are needles in haystacks.**

Most countries, even the United Kingdom, don't really have private universities where students pay their way.

Even Oxford and Cambridge Universities are publicly subsidized. As such, contemplating the prospect of paying at least $30,000 a year in tuition and another $10,000 in room & board, complemented by yet another $20,000 in travel costs, text books and educational supplies, closes out perhaps more than 99% of all international students.

The remaining 1% or so are in a buyer's market and are probably not going to opt for a small, tuition-dependent college in a relatively remote community that is culturally homogenous.

Another problem for smaller, private colleges is being a 'college.'

In most countries of the world, only the designation of 'university' means higher education. 'College' is often a pre-higher education or a vocational school. Most international students seek a university degree, not a college degree. In many countries, the distinction between the two is very significant.

Those who can afford to pay in full usually come from families who are very brand conscious and thereby interested only in the most famous American universities . . .the 'usuals' starting with Harvard, MIT and Yale in the east along with UCLA, USC, Berkeley, and Stanford in the west. Universities with a reasonably recognizable geographic name also have appeal, especially schools like New York University, Boston University, or any California State University or State University of New York.

A large and financially-able contingent of international students, drawn to the prospect of an American university, are already enrolled in a private, high-tuition international school. There are nearly 1,000 such schools throughout the world with names like the American School in London, or in Paris, Geneva, Lugano, Shanghai and virtually every other major world capital. Most of these schools are members of the Council of International Schools and can be identified in their annual directory which can be obtained at www.cois.org.

Families of students enrolled in these schools are accustomed to paying tuition rates that often exceed the rates charged by the most expensive private universities in America. Tuition at The American School in London, a non-residential school, approaches $40,000 annually thanks to an exchange rate, in recent years, that has dropped from $2 per pound sterling to about $1.60. Famed Le Rosey, a school outside Lausanne, Switzerland, is residential and charges a combined tuition, room and board of over $100,000 per year. Both schools, and many others like them, have long waiting lists of full-paying families.

Any tuition-dependent college in America would love to have students from these schools. They have been learning in English for most of their education. Their families can afford private school tuition and have been paying high rates, with minimal to no discounting, throughout their children's lives. However, all these families want their children to attend the most famous and most prestigious universities in America. To attend a small, remotely located college with a name that few, internationally, would likely recognize is a deal breaker. Nothing else such a college may think they have to offer is likely to resonate.

Another potential deterrent is curricular focus. Many small colleges boast their focus on a liberal arts core. While there are many viable and persuasive arguments for the merits of a liberal arts education, they don't as strongly resonate at among many cultures of the world.

Without naming names, many nationalities insist that their children's education be very specifically focused on elite professions.

In some countries, male students have remarkably few acceptable choices, frequently limited to areas like pre-med, engineering and the sciences. Taking even one course outside of such fields of study is viewed as time, money and energy that is wasted. While such families will tolerate the required core curriculum if the university is a Harvard-MIT-Yale class institution, **smaller colleges without an international reputation have virtually no chance of persuading prospective international students that their liberal arts requirements make sense.**

Speaking of academic requirements, **a red flag to avoid is recruiting and enrolling full-paying international students who are academically unprepared and, even, unmotivated to persist through graduation.**

Sometimes the full tuition payment is seductive and is rationalized by the prospect that the student community will become more internationally diverse. Thus, the academically unprepared and unmotivated international student will at least be making a contribution to fellow students by exposing them to a less homogenous student body. Don't do it. Some colleges have made the mistake of enrolling such students in order to strengthen their revenues and have regretted the consequences.

To be blunt, very rich international students with minimal motivation to academically persist contribute nothing of value to their fellow students. Also, they will likely be gone within an academic year, especially if they are in a geographically remote and minimally diverse community.

In summary then, if you are a small, largely-liberal arts institution, are designated a 'college' and are located in a relatively bucolic, non-urban location populated by a largely homogenous culture. . . and, if your motive is largely to find a new enrollment pool of paying students. . .

international students are probably not going to be your silver bullet.

Chapter 8

The Importance of Branding & 'Niche'

"**Ya gotta have a gimmick**" is certainly not, literally, what any college would accept as a tenet that suitably applies to academe. . . especially since the lyric comes from a song performed by burlesque strippers in the Broadway musical, GYPSY. That acknowledged and understood, colleges with niches have an asset that can greatly strengthen their brand name recognition. Any college experiencing shortfalls in enrollment, especially enrollment revenues, should be taking a critical look at the way in which it is presenting itself to the consuming public.

College representatives, from the President down, often find themselves being asked what their college is known for. What sets the college apart? What makes your college unique? What is your college's 'claim to fame.' What is your college's USP (unique selling point(s)?

Every college needs something it can showcase as distinctive, or at least special, when being considered by prospective students and their families.

Whatever it is needn't necessarily be what most students in search of a college are seeking academically, although that would be a double bonus. The distinction, however, has to be something that brings an aura of special quality and status to the institution, thereby providing it with some degree of status and cache.

What doesn't work is any program or attribute that too many other institutions are also presenting as their 'distinction.'

Among smaller undergraduate colleges, the following clichés are typical of over-used characterizations of alleged distinctiveness, or 'niche':

A commitment to excellence
A Faculty who care about their students

Students aren't treated like a number
A College that cares about the individual
A nurturing environment

To put it bluntly, **if your college's 'niche' is a commitment to excellence, your college doesn't have a 'niche.'**

What each college also has to realize is that the distinction that it may consider to be unique may not be of much interest to most prospective students. Many students, frankly, don't want to be nurtured. They see college as their gateway to adulthood and seek the opportunity to spread their wings without being overly monitored.

Some colleges and universities have the good fortune of favorable brand name recognition which in some cases has relatively little, if any, relationship to their academic strengths. How many people can cite the academic flagship(s) of Notre Dame? Yet most everyone knows Notre Dame to be a great academic university that excels far beyond its athletic program.

A remarkably successful initiative was launched by Quinnipiac University just a few decades ago. While a very attractive campus in an accessible location, Quinnipiac had little brand name prestige. Many didn't even know how to pronounce its name. Then, it quite boldly launched a political polling center that has become frequently cited by national news media outlets, particularly during election years when the Quinnipiac Poll has become among the most cited sources of public opinion anywhere. The Poll has become so authoritative that it is now partnered with CBS-TV and *The New York Times*. Now, when a student declares themselves to be a Quinnipiac undergraduate, their affiliation is almost always favorably acknowledged because of the brand name familiarity that the poll has brought the entire University. Yet, when originally conceived, most pundits probably thought that such a poll, to be influential, would have to emanate from a major national university like Yale, Columbia or the George Washington University. Marist College has been equally successful with a poll they launched that is now partnered with NBC News and the *Wall Street Journal*.

Some colleges have the benefit of a great location, and to varying degrees, have incorporated that asset into their marketing and branding. Colleges in major urban centers are especially fortunate as today's college bound students are very drawn to being where the action is and where career accessibility is optimized. In addition to major universities like NYU in Manhattan, GWU in Washington, D.C., Northeastern in Boston, smaller institutions like Emerson in Boston have also grown enormously in recent decades due to their perceived accessibility as much as anything else.

Gettysburg College in Pennsylvania has been greatly strengthened by its presence in a famous Civil War locale that is today a quaint but bustling tourist town charming prospective students and their parents when they visit during their college search. Skidmore College in Saratoga Springs similarly benefits from its residency in Saratoga Springs which continues to be a summer resort for everything from thoroughbred horse racing to symphony orchestra retreats, thereby making the town a similarly exciting place that complements student life at Skidmore. Wagner College in New York catapulted into play when it started showcasing its hilltop campus overlooking the Manhattan skyline and the New York Harbor. Readily accessible to Manhattan, it also offered the bucolic campus atmosphere of a more rural campus thereby offering a quintessential best of both worlds. Drew University, in suburban New Jersey, is a quick train ride away from Manhattan while also being a very centrally accessible bucolic campus. Any college that can make the case of being a great place to spend four years has a cache, of sorts, that will attract students. There are many colleges capable of making a much more compelling case for their location.

Like location, the very aura of the campus can be a marketing plus if, that is, the campus is photogenic, which is much more often the case than is typically showcased by many colleges seeking to attract more students. College admissions experts long ago established that the single-most important event in a college

93

search decision is the campus visit. A 'sale,' or a permanently lost customer, can be determined within the first half hour of a visit. Similarly, many colleges with successful admissions programs will affirm that their most committed applicants were among those students who actually visited. The challenge, though, is enticing prospective students, and their families _to_ visit. With the advent of Internet websites, the ability to show off a beautiful campus has become much easier than it was just a decade or so ago, yet surprisingly many attractive colleges have failed to present their campuses in a way that optimizes the probability that prospective students will want to actually see the campus for themselves.

College websites too frequently present an array of smiling faces who could be from anywhere, giving the viewer little sense of how one college is distinctive from another. Sometimes, the campus photos are remarkably low quality leading one to suspect they were photographed by an admissions counselor on a cell phone camera. Campus maps are sometimes truly unappealing, sometimes just relative crude line drawings, again failing to put the institution's best foot forward.

Every college should have at least a few fundamentally able photographers who know that some of the most beautiful photographs are taken in the early and late hours of the day when the lighting is at its best. Some buildings only get sunlight in the morning, while others in the afternoon. Some of the most appealing moments can be seasonal. . .with fall foliage, with spring blossoms, even with snow.

Colleges could take a page from what real estate agents are now doing to present homes on-line. Some of the more expensive homes are presented very professionally with virtual tours that can be controlled by the website visitor, while, in some cases, even listening to a sound track. Photographers can now mount high-definition television cameras on mini-drone-helicopters not unlike the ones that are sold at high-end hobby stores thereby providing an aerial panorama of the College that improves upon GoogleMap in every way.

Also not showcased frequently enough on-line are facilities that are first rate.

If the college has superior student housing, like townhouses with private bedrooms, there should be photographic evidence on the website. If there is a performing arts center, show it inside and out. The same goes for program specific classrooms, including technology labs. Even the dining hall, if it is appealing, should be included on web pages that are readily accessible.

By now, some professors and deans reading this section have turned beet red protesting that that their college is a place to learn, not a country club or a luxury automobile

for sale...and that academics should be the primary, if not only, reason for college choice. Well, yes, that *should* be the case. And it is the case among families who seek out the 'best' colleges likely to admit their college bound students. Having a strong academic reputation does matter a great deal.

But, among the colleges being considered that do have a good academic reputation, students and their families usually make the final decision based on all facets of the college experience with a heavy emphasis on quality of life.

What WILL it be like to actually live at this college for the next four years? This kind of scrutiny is particularly a major consideration among those students whose families have the financial wherewithal to pay more than 50% of the listed tuition rates.

While even paying students will likely be drawn to colleges they perceive to have the best academic reputation and most prestigious brand name, their final decision when brand name considerations are otherwise equal will be heavily influenced by the supplementary quality-of-life factors.

Speaking of academic reputation, **prospective student families are, alas, heavily influenced by media rankings**. . .especially the *USNews* Best College rating. While these ratings are widely criticized within the higher education profession, and rightfully so, any college struggling with enrollment goals and with net enrollment revenues would be foolhardy to ignore their influence and should insure that accurate data is submitted.

Colleges should also realize that the ratings are heavily weighted by the votes of peer institutions. The presidents, provosts and admissions deans, among others, are polled at all the colleges and universities with which your college is being compared. Almost all of these folks have never visited most of the colleges they are being asked to rate, but that doesn't stop them from casting their votes. While promoting your institution to your colleagues poses no guarantee of winning their vote, colleges need to realize that they will not be cited by any of their peers if they are doing nothing to keep them up to date.

Beyond that, many colleges could do more, especially on their websites, to showcase their "engines" of academic excellence.

Any college with faculty members who are particularly prominent in their field should make

it easy for a website visitor to learn about such professors. Faculty profiles are often buried six or seven layers down into a website and then read like resumes. The pictures of faculty sometimes look like they have been lifted from a driver's license. Faculties who have engaged their students in research, projects, trips or other experiential should be prominently featured.

The same goes for students. Current students and very recent graduates should be showcased as exemplars when they have accomplished something that prospective students might want to emulate…especially if their experiences are not routinely available at other comparable colleges and have opened exciting horizons and opportunities.

Accomplished alumni should be prominently profiled, especially younger successful ones who continue to stay connected to the college and help more recent students get their foot in the door as interns and hires.

These kinds of profiles are perhaps the most compelling arguments that a prospective student can read. Yet it is surprising how infrequently such profiles are prominently featured where web visitors readily find them.

The 'Killer App' Niche

One niche that needn't even be unique (but, for now, probably would be) **belongs to any college that can demonstrate its successful commitment to optimizing the post-graduate outcomes of its undergraduates.**

With nearly half of all college graduates since 2006 without a job related to their college major, or otherwise associated with their career aspirations, prospective students and their families are likely to flock to any college, anywhere, that can show how they are strategically organized to open doors for their students.

So-called 'outcomes' have, in recent years, become more important to colleges, particularly since regional accrediting agencies are including such measurements in their criteria for re-accreditation. Academic, however, have managed to make the case that the outcomes should be largely based on the mission statement of the institution. Many such mission statements are heavily subjective and therefore difficult to quantitatively measure. Such statements as 'preparing our students for a lifetime of learning' doesn't guarantee anything but enlightenment which, while a noble and important outcome, doesn't necessarily pay the rent. Such successful preparation is also hard to measure as an outcome. Not many mission statements, if any, come close to guaranteeing gainful employment in a field related to the college's academic majors.

While most every college has a 'career development' or 'placement' office, many are surprisingly modest in their staffing size given the importance of the outcome, and too often focus on advisement and counseling rather than actual 'match-making.' The typical services of career development offices are too often limited to workshops on how to prepare a resume, or how to dress for a job interview, or even how to eat in a restaurant. Sometimes, the career development office is so remotely located that most students don't even know where it is and only begin seeking it out in their senior year as they approach the end of their college career. Any student waiting that long has squandered valuable years as an undergraduate when important career inroads could have been made.

There was once a time when most employers annually recruited on college campuses. Seniors would go to their career development offices to sign up for interviews resulting, for quite a significant number, in landing a meaningful career start. Perhaps this sort of process is still in effect at the Harvard Business School or at Wharton, not to mention comparable top law schools, but the routine is largely non-existent at undergraduate colleges, thereby perhaps helping explain the 50% unemployment rate among recent college graduates.

Today, access is very restricted to entry level jobs in large numbers of the most sought after careers, especially in areas like media, the arts and major corporate executive training programs. Position openings are virtually never advertised, thereby rendering a resume, as an introductory tool, largely useless.

Those undergraduates aspiring to continuing onward to graduate degree programs needn't be concerned about what they are going to do after they graduate, until, that is, they earn their master's degree or doctorate. Everyone else, though, has to be thinking about their life after graduation, and planning accordingly, almost as soon as they begin their college careers. Too many small colleges, though, have virtually nothing in place that directs students to make such planning one of their top priorities.

Unfortunately, there is some truth in the tenet, 'it's not what you know, but it's who you know.'

There are many who rose to the top, or at least much higher than would otherwise have been the case, because of who they knew and the access to opportunity that those connections brought them. Every opportunity that emerges in a top organization is first known to insiders who will alert a friend's son or daughter, if not their own, thereby giving such privileged offspring a major advantage.

Even when such inbreeding doesn't occur, a modified tenet remains as 'it's not JUST what you know, but also who knows that you know it.'

Opportunities are greatly enhanced when a college student is in the right place to be discovered for the talents that they have and the value they would bring as an employee. One reality that too many colleges don't properly convey to their students is that their years as an undergraduate are the best years to be discovered. If, by the time they graduate, they haven't come to the attention of those who can open doors for the next chapter in their lives, their likelihood of 'landing well' has been greatly diminished.

This is where any college can step to the plate and create a niche that will have many more students beating down their door. Clearly, those colleges near major metropolitan centers have an advantage in being able to match-make their students with prospective future employers. For example, students can volunteer their time as unpaid interns throughout the academic year thereby raising their visibility to those who can 'discover' them.

Speaking of stepping to the plate, this kind of niche creating is where Trustees can play a very powerful enabling role, giving them the opportunity to do more than just ask questions and serve as overseers. **Trustees who are at the zenith of their professional careers can be important enablers, opening doors that give students opportunities they otherwise might never get.**

One of the greatest strengths of the Harvard Business School MBA is the access it grants to B-School alumni in top executive positions. Such is the case for any program that has developed impressive outcomes among its graduates. When an academic program becomes a feeder for rarified career opportunities, its reputation soars as a niche program sought by the most ambitious and able students.

Even more remotely located colleges can fashion together match-making processes that should reach far beyond what Trustees might be able to contribute. Every college has thousands, if not tens of thousands, of alumni. Too often, the college's alumni office focuses its attentions on alumni reunions and giving, without truly immersing alumni in helping currently enrolled students get their post-graduate start.

Some career development offices do run occasional 'alumni career days' where a dozen or so alumni come to the campus and talk about how they got started in their careers.

Perhaps one or two students make a connection that leads to follow-up opportunities, but the majority of students don't experience much of a meaningful outcome. Instead, some portion of the alumni office effort should be directly linked to the student career development effort with the goal of connecting every student, while an undergraduate, to at least one alumnus/a in a related academic/career field. Even if the outcome is a week of mere 'shadowing' alumni in their professional world, the link could be the acorn that becomes an oak tree.

The career development office should be located where students walk by it regularly, perhaps in the student union near food.

The career development personnel should see themselves less as counselors and more as match-makers, working in tandem with the alumni office to find alumni-student match-ups that can work to their mutual benefit.

Moreover, unless the student is certain he/she will be in a graduate school, or they will be working for the family company, or some other career already laid out for them, **all other students should be told that their summers are not best spent backpacking through Nepal or working at a beach concession stand.**

Rather, they should jump at any opportunity, paid or otherwise, to work in a potential career environment where they can perhaps be discovered and even lock up a job commitment BEFORE graduation.

Cooperative education universities, like Northeastern in Boston and Drexel in Philadelphia, have for generations been assigning their undergraduates to "co-op" jobs, often paid, which requires some of their students to spend five years in college, six months in classes and six months on co-op assignment. Although a no-play-and-all-work commitment, this format has consistently resulted in the majority of their graduates being offered full-time jobs after graduation by one of their co-op employers.

Any college, even a liberal arts college, that features such post-graduate match-making (which, over time, generates solid career outcomes for most of its undergraduates) will have a niche that, when combined with solid academic programs, will almost certainly guarantee that motivated college-bound students, and their families, will be flooding the admissions office with applications.

Chapter 9

Attrition, Retention

&

The First Year Experience

A t Board meetings, Trustees are typically presented with quite a bit of detailed data about admissions, although, as previously outlined, sometimes not the data that are most essential to understanding what isn't working, if and when that is the case. Even less information is too often reported about an equally important facet of enrollment revenue; namely, how many students stay and remain through graduation. While "graduation rate," as a percentage, is typically known to Trustees, that rate can be calculated many different ways that obscure the number of students who never really make it that far.

At enrollment revenue dependent colleges struggling to maintain fiscal viability, Trustees should push administrators to have a thorough understanding of why students leave.

Sometimes the circumstances are beyond the control of the institution. Student families can suffer financial setbacks that no longer make private college tuition affordable. Some students experience personal problems that distract them from college studies.

But, there are reasons that can be attributed to institutional failure. First and foremost is admitting students who weren't academically motivated to persist. College admissions offices are disserving the students they admit, and the institution for that matter, when too many students not up to being college students are enrolled. College admissions offices are also at fault if too many of the students they admit aren't really committed to the institution.

As covered in previous chapters, low enrollment yield rates of students admitted can be indicative of an admissions operation that is targeting the wrong students. This strategy not only leads to lower than forecast freshman classes, but classes that are destined to become disproportionately even smaller as each year goes by.

The greatest tragedy, though, is when colleges lose students who were happy to be attending and then don't discover what they had hoped and expected they would find.

The freshman year is the most fragile for student attrition and is often the year least well organized by the institution. Many colleges lose as many as 20% or even more of their freshmen who decide not to return for their second year.

Every time a first year student doesn't return for the second year, the impact is tantamount to giving a 75% refund on what had been a four-year tuition revenue sale.

For a college charging $30,000 a year in tuition, that represents a $90,000 virtual refund on what had been a $120,000 sale.

If a freshman class of 700 students experiences a 20% attrition rate, those 140 departed students, each receiving a virtual $90,000 refund, constitutes $12.6 million dollars in gross enrollment revenue that has been essentially refunded. Even at a school that is discounting at a 50% rate, the loss exceeds $6 million (assuming that the students not returning represented a cross section of the grant aid students enrolled.) In all probability, though, those students who departed, because the institution didn't fulfill their expectations, are students who were probably among those paying a higher rate of the actual tuition, if not 100%. Those students with massive grants, even when dissatisfied, are more inclined to stay because they are unlikely to get comparable grants elsewhere. Where this is the case (and it is more often than not) the average discount rate of upper classes grows beyond the original freshman 50% level. . .a level that was already too high.

When a freshman returns for the sophomore year, and then completes the sophomore year, the probability that this student will continue on through graduation is greatly increased. Therefore, doing *everything* to get first year students deeply rooted in the institution should be of tantamount priority, but too often isn't.

Colleges experiencing high attrition rates often aren't very astute at finding out why students are leaving. While students may be 'required' to officially withdraw, far too many don't accommodate the formalities. They simply don't come back and, once gone, really don't want to spend much time or effort explaining why they didn't stay. Sometimes they don't really know why they didn't stay except to say, usually vaguely, that the college wasn't for them. Many will cite personal or cultural dimensions that didn't click. All this leaves the institution with very little to go on and often has the college officials concluding that the students who departed left for reasons that were not the fault of the college.

"Migratory" and "transitory" are two increasingly commonplace characterizations of today's college student used as a rationale for low retention rates. While it may well be that more college students are attending more than one college during their undergraduate years, that phenomenon may not necessarily be a reflection of a cultural change among today's generation of college students that need be accepted as inevitable. Instead, it may be because today's college students too often opt for the wrong college, or a second-choice college or the college that offered the most grant aid (i.e. discount). Because of this, many more college students today probably begin their college experience at an institution they didn't ideally want to attend.

In part, this troubling trend may well be the result of nationally prominent enrollment consulting firms that have advised colleges to spend most of their financial aid budget on recruiting first year students. These firms are rewarded according to the success rate at the front door, that is, their ability to help colleges yield a large freshman class. Thus, their motivation to channel most of the college's financial aid budget into the freshman year recruits is understandable, albeit not much of anything else.

When students who enrolled because of an attractive financial aid package discover that 'all bets are off' after the first year and that their financial aid thereby disappears, or is massively reduced, they can no longer afford to stay and therefore become "migratory" or "transitory."

Colleges relying upon such 'switch and bait' recruiting methodologies are shooting themselves in the foot and should find ways to locate students committed to staying. They are out there, but are largely not among those students making their decision based on the best financial deal.

Trustees at colleges experiencing high attrition rates who are being told that the low retention is a result of "migratory" and "transitory" student trends should investigate whether the admissions strategies, including non-guaranteed grant aid, are the real culprits.

Look, the fact is that far too much money is being refunded to permit high attrition be rationalized as inevitable.

If each freshman class' attrition results in a $12.6 million loss of potential revenue, three consecutive classes with comparable attrition

can represent over $50 million in revenue loss, each and every student four-year cycle.

That is a lot of money to write off as inevitable and should, therefore, be pursued by Trustees who asked questions that get to the bottom of the problem.

Some colleges have put significant energy into customizing the freshman year in ways that increase the probability that first year students will find what they are looking for and thereby develop a sense of belonging to the institution. While some of the effort is extra-curricular, the most important dimension of these programs is the coursework being offered and the involvement of as many faculty as can be injected into the first year. This approach emerged when some colleges, in trying to improve their freshman year experience, noted that large portions of their faculty had no involvement with first year students. In fact, some entire academic departments were unknown to first year students.

Often, the most senior faculty weigh heavily among those who never teach freshman courses, sometimes because they prefer teaching upper class students more interested in the more advanced facets of their academic discipline. In some cases, keeping such faculty away from first year students might be advisable given their distaste for teaching introductory courses. In many cases, though, too many highly regarded professors never become known to freshman students thereby reducing the student's likelihood of perhaps discovering faculty who 'turn them on' and make them want to return for more.

One model used at many colleges features what are called 'learning communities' where freshman students are clustered into groups of about two dozen students who are overseen by two or three veteran faculty who themselves are part of the learning community. Each faculty group is intentionally academically diverse and comprised of those faculty widely regarded for their accessibility, their teaching effectiveness and, even, their influential seniority. These 'communities' participate in specially crafted multi-disciplinary courses together with a faculty cluster that team-teach the course. At least two such courses, one per semester, are required of all first year students.

The model has proven at many colleges to greatly improve freshman retention into the sophomore year because all students 'belong' to a structured group of fellow students which, it turns out, improves the probability of each student having built bonds which enhance commitment to the college. And, perhaps more important, or at least equally so, freshmen meet a wider array of faculty all of whom are engaged in the learning community beyond the classroom. These communities sometimes get together for out-of-class experiences which occasionally include off-campus experiences and, even, dinners at faculty homes.

113

The faculty members of each community are expected to know all the students in their cluster and to show an interest in each student's individual experience. If something appears not to be going well, they intervene and perhaps even call upon others to help with the problem before it becomes insurmountable.

No college can hope that 100% of first year students will stay on for even the second year, much less four years.

But, colleges are well advised to insure that they are putting their shoulder into the first year experience in order to optimize the number of students in the second year experience.

After all, each freshman retained is $90,000 saved. To paraphrase long-ago U.S. Senator Everett Dirksen, *$90,000 here and $90,000 there and pretty soon it adds up to some real money.* Looked at another way, many colleges spend a fortune in time and money to realize occasional $90,000 donations. Putting that same effort into retaining freshmen could result in many more $90,000 paydays than are likely from donors.

Chapter 10

Athletics

A ny book like this one, which attempts to tackle problems in higher education that most affect small, tuition-dependent colleges struggling with rising costs and declining revenues would be remiss if it didn't comment on athletics. Many smaller colleges faced with budget crises, calling upon them to reduce costs, have often chosen to eliminate sports teams, not because there was a lack of student interest in participating, but because the college viewed the elimination of the sport not a key component of the college education and therefore a prudent cost savings.

115

What perhaps wasn't considered was that the cost savings was offset, if not erased, by the concurrent revenue loss, as many of the participating students then withdraw, moving on to another college where they can continue to enjoy the sports dimension of their college career. In some cases, the revenue loss can far exceed the costs saved.

The most costly sport is football. But, as many as 150 students can be recruited which represents a gross annual enrollment revenue potential of $4 million to $5 million. No NCAA Division II or III football program is costing anything close to that amount. Even if football cost the college $1 million a year, and rarely if ever does it cost anything close to that, the prospect of losing $5 million in revenue in order to save $1 million in spending is not prudent arithmetic.

Non-athletic-scholarship colleges, which constitute most of the audience for which this book has been written, should try to optimize the number of sports they can offer, especially all the sports popular in high schools. Perhaps the most important rationale for this approach is that students involved in team sports are much less likely to leave. **Retention has been shown to be highest among students who are engaged in some sort of group activity outside the classroom.** Sports teams are the most omnipresent, but other groupings like theater companies, musical ensembles and, even, cheerleaders, also prove to root students in ways that greatly increase the probability of their retention through graduation.

This is especially true when it comes to students who are living away from home and who thereby need more than their academic classes to keep them engaged and enthusiastic about the college experience. After all, they are at the college 24 hours a day, seven-days-a-week. Their in-class obligation rarely exceeds 15-hours a week. Even with out-of-class assignments, too much time is left idle if the student is not elsewhere engaged. To avoid the cabin fever that under-engaged students can suffer, especially when attending a relatively remote college, every enrolled student should be on a sports team or engaged in some comparable group undertaking.

Athletic teams can also be a vehicle for gender balance at schools that are disproportionately female. Most smaller residential colleges are more heavily female and some aspire to recruit more males in order to realize balance. Title IX laws complicate the strategy, especially when football is one of the team sports. Over 100 males can be part of a football team and there is no female sport that can come close. In order to comply with gender balance in sports, some colleges wishing to retain their football program find themselves having to eliminate other men's sport, which is a downside of Title IX that couldn't have been intended and should be revisited by federal legislators.

117

But, back to what Trustees need to know about athletics. **Trustees should be reluctant to close down sports programs, or theater programs, or musical ensembles, in the name of fiscal responsibility.** Money will not likely be saved. Money will probably be lost.

Enrollment-revenue dependent colleges should be vigilant and monitor sports programs to insure that coaches are not overly focused on winning teams without meaningful concern for the college's need to be enrolling paying customers.

Unfortunately, college coaches are almost singularly rewarded within their profession for their winning record, even at Division III colleges where there are no athletic scholarships. In order to recruit top athletes without having an athletic scholarship to offer, some coaches focus their recruiting efforts on schools in poor neighborhoods, thereby locating talented athletes who have high financial need and are eligible for large need-based grants, including government funded programs. From the student-athlete's perspective, such a financial aid package is tantamount to an athletic scholarship. While such a strategy may help the coach win games, it doesn't help the college resolve its enrollment-revenue challenges.

Better managed, and rewarded accordingly, coaches need to be redirected to work in tandem with the admissions recruiting program and instead concentrate their recruiting efforts on schools where the athletic recruits can stimulate other students to also apply to the college. Such high schools have to be in economic areas where a meaningful portion of the students come from families financially capable of paying a substantial portion of the tuition, room and board being charged. Coaches who cooperate in this effort will be helping build a network of feeder high schools that can greatly strengthen the college's enrollment and finances.

Colleges with Division II, and especially Division I, programs have the added challenge of managing sports scholarships, which are not permitted in Division III, thereby stimulating some Division III coaches to heavily recruit athletes eligible for need-based aid. While the NCAA has established quantities of sports scholarships that Division II and Division I programs must grant, the College does have some discretion that it should exercise by requiring coaches to be part of the admissions recruiting effort.

Any coach with a winning record, but with a very low graduation rate among team members, is failing the college and should not be retained.

Coaches should all be held responsible to assemble teams of students who are college students first. Coaches should also be working on behalf of the overall mission of the college, recognizing that their sport is a facet of a broad-based experience. They should be helping build feeder high schools where the athletes recruited help serve as a magnet for other students.

The long term positive effects of athletic programs should also be appreciated when contemplating shorter term perceived cost savings. It may take generations, but successful alumni/ae that were part of a sports team, or a theater company, or a band, have a bond that intensifies as the decades go by. Such alumni affinity groups can become major donors who can underwrite a substantial portion of the sports program's costs. It is not unusual to find at least one alumnus/a per sport, for example, who buys uniforms every year or two. . .or equipment.

Trustees should look for cost savings elsewhere and acknowledge the almost essential role that athletics plays in the residential college experience. While there are many academics who think athletics is the first place to look for cut backs, there are many other areas that can be cut without having as adverse an effect on student retention.

Chapter 11

Are all Administrative Staff Positions Really Needed?

One of the principal reasons that small colleges and universities have to charge \$30,000 to \$40,000 or more a year per student is the high cost of running what has become the traditional model of an institution. . .and one that is getting more expensive every year even though the tuition rates now set are probably as high as they can get, if not already over the top. Look at any typical college and it is immediately apparent that the physical plant is impractical. In most eases, there is much more acreage than is needed

121

except from an aesthetic and, perhaps, marketing perspective. Everyone loves to see a beautiful, bucolic campus with lots of stately buildings.

Unfortunately, the maintenance and utilities costs of so many mutually exclusive structures are cripplingly expensive, not to mention the costs of grounds-keeping and, where weather requires, snow removal from hundreds of acres of walkways and roads.

All that said, though, it is unlikely that any college is going to relocate to a more cost-efficient setting.

As expensive as buildings and grounds costs are at many small colleges, none spend as much on physical plant related costs as they do on personnel. Higher education is a labor intensive undertaking and the costs of personnel always consume the largest part of the annual operating budget.

When colleges face having to pare expenditures, the all-too-frequent routine is to impractically call upon all parts of the institution to make cuts, sometimes called 'across-the-board' in the spirit of egalitarianism. Even large universities take this approach which sometimes results in cuts that can have adverse effects on the very sources of revenue, namely students. Harvard may never have to worry about student attrition, which may be why, for a period of time, hot breakfasts were eliminated for undergraduate residents when its endowment was gored by global stock market setbacks.

Smaller colleges facing the need to think more cost-effectively are probably ill-advised to follow Harvard's example by first cutting back on those items, like hot breakfasts, that directly affect student morale.

Reportedly, administrative costs in higher education are growing at a rate faster than any other part of the operating budget.

Such costs can include everything from photocopying to information technology. However, the one area which is probably least scrutinized, especially when it comes to budget cutbacks, is management personnel.

Small colleges have a bad habit of wanting to emulate large universities.

Professors routinely aspire, with the advocacy of their professional associations like the American Association of University Professors (AAUP) to teaching loads comparable to research university professors. Coaches want resources that emulate top sports programs. And, many presidents organize their senior administration as if they were overseeing a major university ten times larger than the college they are actually running. Perhaps this is because too many such presidents were formerly part of a major university infrastructure and cannot adjust to the smaller scale of the college they have joined.

Smaller colleges might be well advised to think twice about hiring anyone from a prominent mega-university who has never worked anywhere else. Sticking with the Harvard comparison, anyone in Harvard's admissions office is not likely to be of much value heading up an admissions office of a small, enrollment-dependent college. There is little that Harvard was doing that resulted in a flood of applications and a 6% acceptance rate that would likely work and generate comparable results elsewhere. And, there are many functions, like marketing, that a smaller college must do but Harvard has never done.

Staffing levels are also not transferrable without potential budget consequences that cannot be sustained by a smaller college. Presidents, provosts and other senior offices at large universities are accustomed to much larger infrastructures that smaller colleges cannot justify. Yet, many senior officers who come to smaller college from larger universities build staffs based on their past experiences.

Once a small college managerial structure is formulated, it is rarely assessed for cost-effectiveness, and certainly not from the perspective of need. Large universities often have academic departments that are larger than some small colleges. Yet, some small colleges staff themselves, particularly at senior administrative levels, as if they were a major university instead of a major university department.

The biggest university-copy-cat can sometimes be the president's office staffing.

Presidents, especially those whose prior experience was largely on the academic side of a university or college infrastructure, and whose expertise is not in management and finance, will often be inclined to surround themselves with executive personnel who can address those areas with which they have limited expertise. Large universities do have substantial staffing in the "Office of the President" that can include:

Chief of Staff
Executive Assistant to the President
Secretary to the Board of Trustees
Assistant to the President for Community Relations
Director of Institutional Planning
Director of Media Relations
Director of Public Relations
Speech Writer
Director of Presidential & Special Events
Assistant to the President/Legal Counsel

Each of these positions, while not uncommon or even unwarranted in major

universities, really has no place in a college of only a few thousand students.

All of these positions, when filled by an executive (as is usually the case) 'requires' a support staff/secretary, and an operating budget. The total cost of this executive cornucopia, including benefits and office costs, can easily approach $2 million annually.

For a student body of 2,000, such unnecessary and often quite expensive positions require each student to be paying as much as $1,000 each in tuition that wouldn't be necessary --- thereby perhaps reducing student debt --- if the positions were eliminated.

A smaller college president's office should be able to manage itself with no more than two support staff personnel, both executive secretarial.

One of the President's executive assistants can handle all administrative duties related to Board governance, major donor relations, community relations and special events. The other can handle the administrative routines of the president's office, including management committees, telephone reception, appointments and correspondence. Presidents should be able to handle their own speeches and external relations work. As for media and public relations, perhaps Harvard has frequent major newspaper, television and related media interest, but most small colleges have but a community newspaper that is sometimes published as infrequently as weekly or monthly.

The most unnecessary position at a small college is Chief of Staff, which is also typically the most expensive.

In a major university, where the president's time falls far short of the obligations and demands placed upon him/her, a chief of staff serves as a chief operating officer. Many academics, most notably Provosts, who become presidents thereby face a whole new set of managerial demands they have never before overseen. In response, they hire a chief of staff to be their alter-ego president. These positions are often salaried in the hundreds of thousands of dollars and, at a small college, duplicate the efforts for which the president had been hired. . .but has delegated. Any president of a small college who has hired a Chief of Staff is spending money that could be much better spent elsewhere. . .or used to lower the tuition being charged to the students and their families.

Examples of management inflation within the academic hierarchy are also commonplace. Large universities typically have an academic infrastructure that is topped by a Provost and Vice Provost, followed by Deans, followed by Faculty Chairs/Department Heads. Sometimes there are several Associate Provosts for assignments like accreditation and institutional assessment.

Any college in the 2,000 student range doesn't need Schools, Deans <u>AND</u> Faculty Chairs.

Some small colleges have created Deans for 'schools' that are staffed by fewer than ten faculty members serving fewer than 200 students. No Dean should be overseeing any 'school' that enrolls under 500 students with fewer than two dozen faculty. There is no established rule from which these numbers have been culled. Just common sense.

Small colleges cannot spend like large universities. They simply cannot afford to staff up to the level of institutions with enrollments and operating budgets that are ten times larger.

My first act as President is to appoint retired General Stone
to the newly created position of Chief of Staff. General Stone
will manage the President's Office and will oversee
all campus management functions thereby
freeing me up to focus my time elsewhere.

Chapter 12

The Importance of Bricks, Mortar & Ivy

A s already cited, the on-campus visit plays a powerful role in college-choice . . . and the single-most important facet of that campus visit is the condition of the campus and the facilities. From the student's perspective, the question is whether everything feels like the kind of place to spend the next four years. Parents are probably trying to determine whether the college feels like the kind of place that justifies the cost.

From the college's perspective, the campus has to be competitive with other colleges that are being visited by the prospective student and family.

Some colleges can shoot themselves in the foot without even realizing it. Litter, unkempt grounds, external disrepair can send a message that the college is not well managed. If they don't even care about picking up litter, what else are they ignoring that is more important?

These assessments are most likely to be incorporated into the decision making process of the college's most desirable applicants. . .namely, paying customers. Students in search of the largest scholarship will probably overlook campus conditions as they can only afford to attend the most financially generous. But, no tuition-dependent college can afford to be attracting only the financially needy. Someone has to pay for those discounts, so un-endowed colleges have to look to full paying students to essentially underwrite those students who are attending for less than the full tuition rate.

Most Boards of Trustees have some semblance of a Buildings & Grounds subcommittee which, when possible, is staffed with Trustees who know something about real estate, construction and, nowadays, technology. These committees typically tour the campus at least once a year and should be able to get a sense of where improvements are needed. However, most Presidents insure that the campus is at its best on the two or three times a year when Boards of Trustees convene, so they may not be seeing how the college more routinely presents itself.

More important, though, is something that Trustees often don't do, and that is visiting the competition. Any college experiencing enrollment shortfalls should be studying what successful competitors are doing. The fact is that student families with financial wherewithal typically apply to at least five colleges and visit them all. With the exception of name brand prestige, which prevails as the most compelling influence on college choice, all other things being relatively equal, the reaction to the campus and its resources will be the strongest influence among those in the position to decide without consideration of price.

Therefore, some Trustees, including those on the Executive Committee, should annually set aside time to tour other colleges that tend to 'cross-app' with your college. Cross-app simply means those colleges that most frequently are among the other colleges that most applicants also apply to, and, even more importantly, choose instead of your college.

The tour should include a visit to student residences, but also classrooms, labs and recreational buildings. Many colleges are just not keeping up with the competition and are paying the price without knowing it.

Many colleges with enrollment revenue shortfalls have actually been cutting back on physical plant maintenance and improvements instead of cutting elsewhere, like in over-staffed administrations, or under-enrolled academic programs, or on fund-raising programs that are costing more than is being raised.

As any business executive who is a Trustee could affirm, if the product isn't selling, you don't spend less on it, you improve it so it will sell better. Too many Boards too hastily call for spending cuts when revenues drop. In doing so, they also too often cut in the wrong areas with physical plant almost always being at or near the top of the list. Boards should think twice before such cuts, especially if they have never visited the campuses of the most successful competition.

Any college without a competitive campus and educational resources needs to set investment in those resources as the first and foremost priority. Some Boards, with Presidential concurrence, have mistakenly focused on endowment instead of physical plant and, in doing so, are potentially impairing their competitiveness. Endowment should become a priority only after all expenditures affecting the successful attainment of enrollment revenue goals have been fulfilled.

Chapter 13

Is Anyone Assessing Faculty?

F aculty are to colleges what doctors represent to hospitals or what pilots are to airlines. Boards of Directors of hospitals are not really in the position to evaluate the performance of brain surgeons and most Board members of airline companies have never flown a plane, so are certainly not in the position to rate pilot skills. Similarly, most college trustees lack academic doctorates, are not research scholars and have never taught a college course. As such, many, if not most, if not all, college professors would assert that the Board of Trustees has no role in evaluating their effectiveness. Instead, faculties should self-assess because 'it takes one to know one.' There is logic in that tenet just as only another surgeon can really assess the competence of a fellow surgeon. That being the case, faculty are largely in charge of hiring professors, evaluating them and granting them tenure. Provosts and department heads play an administrative role in the process, but virtually all such college officers are themselves professors. Faculty also prevail, almost always without Board oversight, in what courses are taught, what books are read, what materials are covered and how students are assessed.

In many respects, and perhaps properly so, trustees tend not to want to get involved in the details of the curriculum, or of faculty credentialing. At most, trustees will receive periodic overviews that include ratifications of faculty tenure which are not really subject to Board challenge, thereby making the ratification a virtual rubber stamp.

Because 'academic freedom' is a national standard, strongly heralded by the American Association of University Professors (AAUP), no smaller college stands a chance, really, of challenging the norms which strongly defend the unilateral and independent prerogatives of faculty. Those prerogatives are unlike any other profession. For instance, are faculty management or employees? The AAUP assertively supports the role of faculty in institutional governance while at the same time advocating faculty rights to employee collective bargaining. The AAUP seems to resist being portrayed as a labor 'union', but defends member 'rights' in about the same way that any traditional labor union does. Their website heavily focuses on issues of faculty workload, faculty compensation, collective bargaining, academic freedom and discrimination. Student outcomes, teaching evaluations, performance measurements and similar standards of academic quality have a lesser presence on the website.

Vital Signs of Tenure

Tenure is something that no small college can successfully challenge. It is a national sacred cow that will change only when the major national universities take a lead in modifying its principles. Nevertheless, the problems it creates should at least be understood by Trustees.

Before getting into tenure, the nature of the professoriate is worth considering and understanding. While every college and university can showcase wonderful professors who are absolutely dedicated to their undergraduate students, every college is saddled with at least a few tenured faculty who don't like teaching undergraduates all that much, especially those undergraduates who don't aspire to major in the faculty member's academic discipline.

The profession of professor may be unique in that, among other things, there is no training required in teaching to be hired to do exactly that. Professors are hired based on their knowledge of a subject. . .knowledge that is expected to be of the highest levels of scholarship, far exceeding anything necessary to teach at the college undergraduate level. Earning a Ph.D. in any discipline requires a very advanced knowledge of that discipline that more appropriately has a role in education at the master's and doctoral levels.

Nowhere has it ever been proven that possessing expertise in an academic discipline means that one is thereby capable of conveying that knowledge to anyone else. Yet, all colleges and universities are more or less faced with having to presume that to be the case.

Many. . .a very large many. . .of those who earn Ph.D.'s in a discipline pursued that degree because of their interest in the subject or field, and not because they had any interest in teaching others, especially teaching young undergraduates with limited interest in the subject but who must take the course in order to fulfill a core curriculum requirement.

Upon earning their Ph.D., many scholars aspire to become professors because the career path is among the few that permits them to continue their scholarship, their research and their publications. Teaching, especially teaching introductory subjects in an undergraduate environment, is a necessary evil that comes with the territory. As such, many scholars who become professors look forward to the day when they can at least amass the seniority that permits them to limit their teaching obligations to those students aspiring to earn Ph.D.'s in that same discipline. The prospect of teaching freshman and sophomore courses (often termed 'service' courses) for an entire career is, for many, a sentence worse than death.

Faculty in major research universities that offer master's and doctoral degrees are able to move up into the graduate programs and, as they amass seniority and rank, can avoid teaching undergraduates altogether. However, faculty who are life-tenured in small undergraduate colleges with virtually no graduate-level degree offerings, are subjected to teaching basic courses for their entire career. This is one of the downsides of tenure which poses a problem both for the faculty members who earn it and for the institutions forced to grant it.

Along with some labor unions, higher education's tenure process has to be among the few career paths where one is guaranteed a job for life, with minimal accountability, after only seven years on the job. Most Ph.D.'s are earned by scholars in their mid-to-late twenties when, if fortunate, they are hired as Instructors or Assistant Professors on what is called a tenure track. Then, those who successfully work themselves through the seven year gauntlet of their first job can find themselves awarded a set of golden handcuffs in their early 30's. . .thereby guaranteeing them their job for perhaps the next half century or even longer. From the time of earning tenure, and for the next four, or five, or six decades, the tenured professor's performance as a teacher is largely untouchable. Only if they never show up for class, are demonstrably dysfunctional, or are breaking a moral or legal standard, can they been challenged. As they amass seniority, they can select, and sometimes even create, the courses they teach while declining those they disdain. . .like, all too often, introductory freshman courses.

In smaller undergraduate colleges, there is no other career advancement for professors.

In fairness, many small colleges can rightly and proudly boast of veteran faculty who knew what they were getting themselves into, were scrutinized during the first seven years for their commitment and effectiveness in teaching undergraduates, and have remained productive and highly regarded throughout their decades of teaching basic undergraduate courses year after year, decade after decade. Such professors are often showcased by their affiliated colleges as exemplary, but do not necessarily represent their majority of their colleagues.

139

At major universities, veteran professors can rely upon master's and doctoral students to serve as teaching assistants who often carry a major proportion of the basic course teaching load assigned to the professor. At smaller undergraduate colleges, such graduate student populations don't exist although veteran faculty often develop the same lack of interest in their introductory courses to the disservice of the first and second year students.

Every college has a different relationship with its faculty, but virtually all do comply with AAUP standards for academic freedom which include an expansive array of prerogatives that arguably have little to do with the fundamental tenet of academic freedom.

How many courses should be taught per semester, for instance, is a workload issue not related to academic freedom. Rewards for merit are also not academic freedom related, but are typically opposed by faculty who contend that any criteria established to reward meritorious faculty will be abused by management and governance (i.e., Trustees) to punish faculty who criticize institutional leadership and reward those who acquiesce.

Workload itself is an area not really related to academic freedom, but it is nevertheless clustered with academic freedom rights over which management and governance have relatively limited control. The annual faculty workload obligation can, in many cases, be remarkably small as compared to just about any other profession, or non-profession, in America or elsewhere.

A full-time college professor's central obligation is teaching courses, and, of course, the preparation and follow-up which includes evaluations and grading. While there is always some tweaking and updating, class preparation, over time, can become less demanding for those professors who teach the same courses year after year, especially course like history where content remains relative static from decade to decade as compared to, say, information technology which changes almost daily. The work for many faculty members can be redundant as the years go by, which even some professors will acknowledge.

About the heaviest teaching load facing a full-time professor is four courses per semester, each course meeting about three hours per week. In such maximum teaching-load circumstances, the in-class weekly obligation totals twelve hours a week, leaving 28 hours in a 40-hour work week remaining for other obligations like student advising, marking papers and tests, committee meetings, etc.

There are indeed many college professors, particularly non-tenured ones, who busily fill the non-classroom hours with legitimate work associated with the needs of the college and its students. Other professors, often those who have been tenured for decades, are not

141

always as omnipresent. Some faculty, and no one knows how many, reach a level of independence and seniority where they can teach the courses they wish, where and when they wish. These same faculty sometimes cluster all their weekly teaching obligation into three, or, sometimes, only two weekdays. Tuesday and Thursday classes of one-and-a-half hours each can fulfill the entire week's obligation for a course, thereby leaving Monday and Friday with no teaching obligation. Wednesday can be set aside for student advising hours and committee meetings. And, Monday and Friday can be off campus permitting four-day weekends.

Faculty who have assembled something comparable to this work routine will often insist that their four-day weekends are used for scholarly purposes like research, journal articles, books and other professional endeavors that add to the academic stature of the college while also keeping the professor academically 'current' and therefore a better teacher. In some cases, that is true. In other cases, it is not. Usually, though, colleges do little to monitor who is in the former and who is in the latter category.

While college professors cite themselves as full-time employees of the college earning full-time annual wages, they sometimes contradict that tenet when being called upon to do anything at the college that doesn't occur during the weeks when the college is in session for the fall and the spring semesters.

Our Econ professor is tenured so he has
something called academic freedom. He came to
the opening class to introduce his teaching assistants
and he'll be returning for a lecture sometime next week.

The fall semester of courses, at most colleges, begins in September and ends in mid-December. This is a span of about 15 weeks, not counting a fall mid-semester break and a Thanksgiving break. The winter-spring semester begins in late-January and ends, usually, in mid-May. Not counting the spring mid-semester break, this comprises another 15-week teaching obligation. Together, these two semester represent about 30-weeks of teaching contact that many, if not most, college faculty consider to be their total annual workload obligation. Therefore, the other 22 weeks outside the fall and spring semesters are considered by many college professors to be their own time to do whatever they want. Their annual salary, that is, covers only the 30-weeks of the fall and spring semesters.

Any professor teaching additional courses, say in the summer, is compensated additionally in most cases, thereby representing the college's agreement that their annual full-time salary did not include any work outside the fall and spring semester span of 30 weeks. Thirty weeks is 58% of a full year and 63% of the full year that all other employees of the university are obligated to work. As many non-faculty college employees would be quick to note, they receive no additional pay for summers or any other time, including January (when classes are not in session but the offices of the college, except faculty offices, are otherwise open and busy).

For 2011-2012, the AAUP cited the average salary of a full professor at a smaller, baccalaureate college to be $101,568 and an Associate Professor to be $75,106. These salaries are typically compared to administrators who, faculty advocates often complain, make more when it is the faculty who are the lifeblood of the institution. If indeed, faculty must be compensated additionally for any work done for the college outside of the two semesters, the 63% of time which their full-time salary covers would, on an annual equivalent basis take a full professor's $101,560 salary to $161,219 thereby exceeding the annual full-time salary of small college Provosts, cited by the *Chronicle of Higher Education* for 2012-2013 as being $149,000. And, that doesn't take into account those faculty who are on campus fewer than five days a week.

As already observed, there is not a lot, if anything, that Presidents and Trustees can do about the way in which a college professor's salary and work expectations have been established.

The major universities are going to have to take the lead on issues of accountability and even *they* may not succeed.

Nevertheless, Board members should occasionally be asking about faculty workloads

if only to understand whether a problem exists, or doesn't exist.

Without naming names of faculty, Trustees could be given a presentation of course offerings illustrated by day of the week and hour of the day. If course loading is heaviest in the middle of the week and comparatively miniscule on Mondays and Fridays, the long-weekend syndrome may be in effect in ways that do not serve students well. If, for example, too many faculty have loaded their course obligations on the same day, students can't get into courses that are offered at the same time. At smaller colleges, where some required courses are only offered once a semester, this kind of overcrowding can prevent students from graduating on time.

Again, without naming names, Trustees should be able to ask how many professors are scheduled in the classroom for five days a week, four days a week, three days a week, or fewer.

Trustees should also have a sense of student workload per faculty member. Colleges like to boast small class size as a plus in instruction and learning, and faculty would be the first to agree. What are, though, the total number of students per faculty member per semester. If the full-time work load is four courses and the average class size is 15 students, each faculty member should average 60 students per semester. In this model, how many faculty teach more than 60 students. . .how many teach fewer than 50. . .how many teach fewer than 40. . .how many teach fewer than 30. . .and so on. Also of interest might be a breakdown of faculty rank by category. Not untypically, junior untenured faculty teach massive first year courses while veteran, tenured faculty teach under-populated senior seminars.

In the short run, data like these probably can't result in any action, but, over time, it may reveal academic programs that don't have student interest and perhaps shouldn't exist. It may also reveal excessive underutilization of faculty resources that can at least be brought to the attention of the faculty with a call for them to self assess the situation.

National standards for faculty accountability and obligation make it very difficult for individual small colleges to disregard or otherwise successfully challenge any of the faculty self-governance rights, including tenure.

Nevertheless, trustees should maintain a watchful vigil over processes like tenure recognizing that the college is locking itself into costs over which they will have virtually no control for decades and even generations going forward.

Every time trustees grant just one tenure award, they have locked the college into a $2 million - $5 million, or even more, expense.

147

Colleges remain obligated to grant tenure to full time faculty, which is a job for life, after less than a decade on the job. As such, many faculty become tenured while in the early 30's. As there is no longer a legally enforceable retirement age, being granted tenure at such a young age secures guaranteed employment for fifty years or more.

If young untenured faculty are routinely renewed annually during their first five or six years on the job, without meaningful critiques of shortfalls in their performance, the prospect of denying tenure is almost impossible to legally defend. Knowing they will be faced with tenure recommendations annually as younger faculty reach their eligibility date, Trustees should be fully aware of what steps are being taken annually to insure that potentially weak faculty are not being routinely renewed thereby obligating the college to grant tenure when the eligibility year arrives.

Trustees should also know the criteria being employed for evaluating younger faculty. Often, even at undergraduate colleges where teaching effectiveness should be tantamount, faculty committees can focus their evaluations on research and scholarship achievement rather than insuring that younger faculty are being assessed heavily for their effectiveness teaching undergraduates long with their likely willingness to be focused on that component of their job for the next half century.

Once tenured, professors who are not all that interested in teaching undergraduates are largely untouchable and the college is faced with an annual expense that will never go away. Additionally, tenured faculty who hang onto their jobs for four or five decades make it impossible to hire new and energized younger faculty, sometimes for generations at a time.

Granting tenure is a very big decision that shouldn't be rubber stamped by trustees.

Chapter 14

Can Trustees Question Instructional Costs?

T rustees, and even presidents and provosts, have
for decades, if not generations, fundamentally
avoided confronting the assessment of instruction
even though instruction has become more costly
than most families can afford to pay. Each year,
as costs have risen, the solution has been to raise tuition
rather than manage costs. That approach has pretty much
run its limit and colleges must now face having to look for
ways to do more for less.

In the years ahead, Trustees and presidents, especially those overseeing tuition-dependent institutions, are going to have to look everywhere for cost effective solutions aimed at not only minimizing cost increases, but reducing the current level of expenditure. When it comes to involuntary costs, like health insurance for staff, reducing premium costs may require a reduction in the quality of the benefit. Lowering the electric and fuel bills will require similar cutbacks in the quality of life that could adversely affect morale that in turn could impair productivity.

Before such Draconian steps are undertaken, every other dimension of the traditional way in which colleges have operated should also be studied. The most sacred of these cows is the faculty and the cost of instruction. Very little performance data are routinely submitted to the Board, or, for that matter, the president. . .especially such data that relate to cost.

Faculty, along with academic leaders (i.e., Provosts, Faculty Chairs, Deans) have successfully made the case that instruction cannot be, and should not be, assessed from a cost-effective perspective. In some respects, they are right. It is much less expensive, for instance, to teach a 30-student class studying history than teaching those same 30 students a course like chemistry or physics. The costs of science labs, art studios and engineering workshops result in per student

151

costs that go through the roof when compared to teaching students how to write well. To thereby make a decision to cut back on the sciences and schedule more low-cost writing courses isn't a sound way to manage a college curriculum.

Any Trustee questioning the costs of college instruction also faces being labeled a Philistine unsuited to the role of college overseer. This accusation has often arisen, for example, when Trustees advocate curricular directions aimed at training students for a specific career. Faculty throughout the arts and sciences passionately defend the role of the liberal arts in higher education, and understandably so.

A compelling case has been made, and is long standing, for the importance of broad based knowledge regardless of what profession or career track one takes. Virtually all colleges, therefore, offer what they typically promote as an essential core curriculum of liberal arts subjects aimed at providing all students, regardless of major, with a foundation that assures graduates are well read, are articulate, can speak and write well, have an appreciation for the arts, an understanding of the sciences, of human behavior, of history, and so on.

While no one is likely to succeed in arguing against the teaching of this core knowledge. . .and no one *should* succeed. . .the existence of this common liberal arts core has been the seed of many operational and financial problems that have contributed to the financial problems that smaller, tuition dependent colleges today face. Most typical is when faculty teaching the core become tenured and use their senior rank to avoid the tedium of continuing to teach freshman and sophomore core courses, thereby requiring the college to hire junior adjuncts to do the work that more senior professors no longer wish to undertake. When this happens, operating costs go up while student enrollments remain stable.

Too many majors?

Smaller colleges sometimes offer too many academic majors, thereby arguably impairing quality that would be enabled if limited resources were directed, in larger amounts, to fewer majors.

When small colleges tries to do too much, as is often the case, they spread their resources too thinly thereby disserving students and potentially causing increases in student attrition as better students transfer to other colleges where their major is better staffed.

The 1,500 colleges to which this book is dedicated are all faced with being too small to be all things to all people.

Nevertheless, the pressure to offer too many majors is intense, especially from faculty and admissions personnel, which can too often prevail over the practical wisdom of quality vs. quantity.

There is an understandable, albeit inadvisable, rationale for establishing too many majors. The admissions offices of smaller colleges, that must aggressively pursue prospective new students every year, don't want to turn away *any* student expressing an interest in the institution. Therefore, any major not offered, that is being sought by any prospective student, too often becomes a proposed new major advocated by the admissions recruiters in order to achieve enrollment goals.

Any resistance to adding academic majors becomes an excuse, of course, for poor admissions results.

The faculty can be as intense a stimulus for new majors, but not necessarily because there is a demand among prospective students. Without a major in, say, American History, those professors hired to teach history are 'doomed' to a career where the courses they teach are forever relatively introductory ones that form the liberal arts core required of all students regardless of major.

Teaching the same introductory courses semester after semester, year after year,

decade after decades, is a bleak prospect for any faculty member who has earned a Ph.D. in an academic discipline that is no more than a "service" course in the core curriculum.

The opportunity, instead, to teach advanced courses in history, to students, who, like them, love the discipline, is a very appealing prospect but is only possible if there are students majoring in the subject.

As a result, many small colleges bite off more than they can chew, by offering too many majors, too often in response to appeals from the admissions office and from ranking faculty in disciplines that are not yet offered as majors.

Take one small, tuition-dependent college in the rural east that, to protect confidentiality, will be called Irving College. Irving is located in a small town hours away from any major urban center and enrolls about 1,200 under-graduates. The full-time faculty totals fewer than 100. Irving portrays itself as a liberal arts college, as do far too many of the 1,500 institutions for which this book has been written. Contrary to their liberal arts claim, two-thirds of the students major in business, education and health care. . .mostly business. Because of its location, Irving struggles to enroll and retain students and, in an attempt to do so, offers over thirty-six majors including in all the liberal arts subjects that form the core curriculum.

With over three dozen majors being taught by fewer than 100 full-time faculty, the average number of faculty per major is fewer than three. Many of the majors have only one or two faculty. Having spread themselves so thinly, the heavily enrolled majors, like business, have too few professors to serve the students who are majoring in business. Even though 50% of the students are majoring in business, less than 10% of the faculty teaches business. This results in business faculty being overloaded with disproportionate numbers of advisees while the faculty of minimally-enrolled majors has a much lighter work load.

Some majors at Irving, like criminal justice, have but one faculty member. As a result, those students majoring in criminal justice face taking most, if not all, of their criminal justice courses from the same faculty member. That isn't good for the student, who is denied the breadth and depth that a variety of criminal justice faculty would provide. Many students serious about the discipline might transfer to a larger institution where they can receive a broader and deeper advanced program of instruction.

Adding majors can also be much more expensive than originally promised by the proposing faculty.

At one small mid-Atlantic college, a veteran chemistry professor made the case for adding a chemistry major insisting that the additional senior level courses would require little more than some instructional time that was available largely within the underutilized existing tenured faculty. The major was approved, although it never drew a significant number of students.

Within a year or two after the major was in place, that same veteran chemistry faculty member appealed for accreditation from the American Chemical Society. No chemistry major will be taken seriously, he contended, if enrolled in a program that was without such accreditation. However, the American Chemical Society required that all accredited programs subscribe to their annual Chemical Abstracts publications. These abstracts were collections of very esoteric research papers, penned by college and university chemistry faculty, thereby helping faculty improve their publications portfolio. . .often a requirement for tenure.

The subscription cost for the abstracts, which no undergraduate, even chemistry majors, would ever be likely to read, was tens of thousands of dollars a year and took up library shelf space in what was a relatively small library. The only positive outcome of adding the chemistry major was to give senior faculty a small cadre of students to whom they could teach upper level courses and thereby avoid a career otherwise limited to introductory material. An inspection of the chemistry abstracts shelved in the library revealed that none of them had ever been used, even by the faculty members.

The problem is intensified in the liberal arts core subjects, like history and literature, where the full-time tenured faculty hired to teach the core courses are now teaching upper class courses thereby requiring additional adjunct faculty to teach the freshman and sophomore core.

Trustees are minimally involved in approving new majors as they are often launched by faculty committees with the approval of senior management. Colleges should establish some measurable ground rules before introducing an academic major. First and foremost, there should be a minimum number of professors in the discipline to insure that students have access to the breadth and depth of expertise they have a right to expect. No student should be subjected to a major where only one or two professors teach all upper class courses in the major. Also, there should be an agreed-upon minimum number of majors enrolled in both the junior and the senior classes. If fewer than two-dozen juniors, and another two-dozen seniors cannot be found for the major, it should be eliminated and the faculty should redirect their attention to first and second year students.

Trustees and presidents need to understand to what degree the courses and majors being offered are adversely affecting the institution's viability.

Smaller colleges might be best advised to focus on fewer academic areas that they can deliver exceptionally well with proven results.

Vital Signs of Instructional Cost

Trustees should be seeking to know more about the relative size and cost of each major offered.

With a total undergraduate enrollment of 1,200, at least 300 and probably more like 400 of the students are freshmen and therefore are not yet majoring. Therefore, no more than 800 students are majoring in the 36 majors being offered at Irving College. As nearly two-thirds are in three of the majors, business, education and health care, 33 majors are serving the other one-third of those 800 students, or no more than 300 students. That comes to fewer than ten students per major. . .spread among sophomore, junior and senior classes.

Ten students per major, per year, are too few for any college to justify the costs of providing the upper-class courses required in each specific discipline. In all probability, Trustees are rarely shown the class loads by upper-class discipline and should therefore at least occasionally ask for this information.

Trustees should also know the specific advisee loads of faculty by discipline, not the average number of advisees.

At some institutions, student majors in heavily enrolled disciplines, like business, are assigned faculty advisors who are not part of the business faculty. Such assignments, while more fairly distributing the advisee load, don't serve students effectively and can contribute to attrition when students transfer to other institutions where their major is more suitably staffed.

Trustees are often given data about average class size, but that average can be misleading if the real class sizes are widely skewed. Instead, **Trustees should ask for class sizes by introductory core courses and by each major. . .at the very least.**

While faculty may resist the release of such information, **the student load by faculty member can be a very revealing number that is rarely reported.**

Vital Signs of Faculty Workload

As already pointed out, some professors have been very effective in carving out a role in the governance of the institution that insulates them from scrutiny, particularly from Trustees who inquire about performance measurements. Such quantitative benchmarks are challenged as being anti-intellectual and contrary to the scholarly nature of the professoriate. Faculty will self-assess and be subjected to peer assessment that is ongoing, so goes the argument. No one else understands the profession and should stay out.

However, now that the cost of higher education has reached the overload level, Trustees are obligated to look at all major expenses, including the comparative statistics that illustrate the relative cost of teaching.

The inescapable reality is that the traditional ways of organizing the instructional system, including faculty work load, have to change.

There is no widely accepted standard for acceptable faculty work load. At one time, there existed what seemed to be a relatively common workload of four courses per semester, two semesters per year. Each course met three to four times a week for about an hour per meeting. The standard class size, at least at smaller colleges, rarely exceeded 30 students.

Faculties at many colleges have been successful in making the case for reducing their semester course load to fewer than four courses per semester. They have argued that their scholarly obligations, along with other responsibilities placed upon them, like committee and advising loads, takes too much of their time to also be called upon to teach four courses. . .even though four courses meeting three to four hours a week adds up to 16 hours of contact time, less than half the proverbial 40-hour-work week that very few professionals enjoy in a world that now typically demands 60-hours or more.

Trustees are not likely to succeed in establishing a minimum standard for the number of courses taught, nor the minimum number of students. But, they should at least have the information provided to them in more detail than a shrouded institutional average.

Every Trustee should read,

HOW COLLEGES ARE WASTING OUR MONEY AND FAILING OUR KIDS --- AND WHAT WE CAN DO ABOUT IT, a book written by Andrew Hacker, a well-known college professor emeritus from CUNY Queen's College in New York City, who frequently writes for *The New York Times*, and co-authored by Claudia Dreifus.

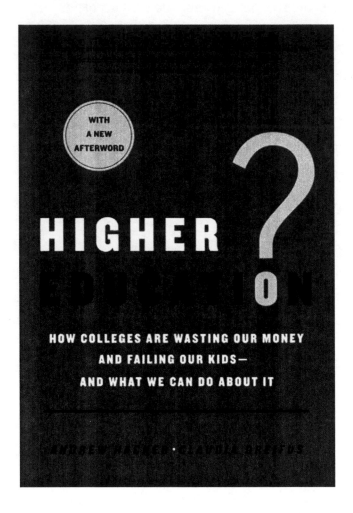

Hacker's book details how most American institutions of higher education are spending far too much of undergraduate tuition revenues on expenses that don't serve the undergraduates who are paying for them, most notably for research, but also for unnecessary administration infrastructures. The book focuses on major universities, but it is those major universities that too many smaller colleges unrealistically attempt to emulate in their organization and practices. Not surprisingly, Hacker's book has not always been well received by college professors and academics. However, the book has been lauded by many major university presidents and by nationally regarded book reviewers.

Chapter 15

Is There a Role for Trustees in Accreditation?

Many college trustees will report that they know very little about accreditation and that it rarely, if ever, comes up at Board meetings. To some degree, no news is good news. Accreditation, really, is only a serious issue when the college is in jeopardy of losing it. What is accreditation? Well, it is pretty much what the name says it is. Namely that an accredited college has the veritable "Seal of Good Housekeeping" that gives students and their families assurances that they are investing in a credible educational institution. Accreditation is to higher education what an S&P rating is to corporation finances, what an FDA approval is to drugs and, perhaps to a less confidence-building extent, what a Better Business Bureau rating is to consumer services.

It would take a rather large book to fully brief Trustees on accreditation, so this brief chapter will highlight a few key basics, including some suggestions where Trustees might be well advised to monitor activity and outcomes.

While there are myriad accrediting agencies for an array of academic disciplines and professions, the giants in higher education are the regional accrediting bodies of which there are five, dividing the country and, for that matter, the world, into five groupings: New England, Middle States, North Central, Southern and Western.

Each of these regional bodies is overseen by a Board of Commissioners, a largely self-perpetuating body of mostly higher education officers and academics from member institutions within the region represented. Some federal and state legislators, among others, have been critical of these commissions accusing them of being inbred and thereby lacking the objectivity to critical assess their peers. The Commissioners are volunteer positions but there is a paid administrative staff for each commission comprised of dozens of professionals who manage and coordinate the

evaluation and accreditation processes overseen by the
Commissioners.

Every college and university seeking accreditation
from these regional commissions (which is just about every
college and university within each region from the top Ivy
League schools to the smallest of two-year colleges) is
subjected to a once-a-decade, on-campus evaluation visit.
The on-campus evaluation team is coordinated by a staff
member of the Commission along with a group of
administrators and faculty members from other colleges and
universities within the region. The team is usually chaired
by a college or university president. All the team members,
with the exception of the Commission staff liaison, are
volunteering their time on leave from their college. Some
consider it an honor to be tapped as an evaluator. Many
presidents dread serving as being comparable to grand jury
duty.

**The reason that many Trustees feel they
know little about accreditation may be good
news.**

If the Commission evaluation team likes what it sees
during its on-campus evaluation (which usually lasts two to
three days), they will submit their evaluation report
affirming their favorable assessment. Upon receipt of the
report, the Commissioners will grant a reaccreditation for

another decade and that is the last you will hear from the Commission except for a mid-decade status report submission which can be an uneventful routine. That's when everything is up to accreditation standards and there are no shortfalls in fulfilling accreditation criteria.

If, however, the evaluation team finds shortfalls in the criteria established to qualify for accreditation, the college can be subjected to troubling and burdensome setbacks and adversities that can seriously impair enrollment. Especially since the advent of the Internet, information about accreditation is much more readily available than had been the case previously. Any college facing scrutiny because of shortfalls in accreditation compliance can now be found on the accrediting commission's website.

Failures to comply with standards, depending on their seriousness, can result in probation and even removal of accreditation, the latter being tantamount to closing down the college.

As such, removal of accreditation is a rarity, perhaps too rare in the opinion of some lawmakers who have been demanding a more severe scrutiny of colleges and universities.

The first warning that something is wrong comes immediately after the Commission's review of the on-campus evaluation. If the report cites serious compliance failures, the first step of the Commission will be to issue some kind of conditional accreditation that calls upon the college to 'show cause' or to get to work on correcting the violations. Usually, the college will be called upon to submit a report within a year showing satisfactory progress toward compliance. Even then, the accreditation could continue to be conditional calling upon the college to submit annual reports each year until compliance is achieved.

Failure to show satisfactory progress can result in probation. Probation means nothing more than having to wear a virtual Scarlet Letter on the Commission website, but such a stigma can have serious repercussions for a college already experiencing fragile enrollment outcomes. Prospective students will very likely be deterred from pursing enrollment at a college with probationary status.

Losing routine reaccreditation can also become a burdensome and costly addition to an already strained operating budget.

The college must pay all the travel costs, accommodation costs and staff costs of on-campus visits. When they become annual, they can add costs the college cannot afford. Moreover, the amount of staff time required to organize all the materials that accreditors demand can be very distracting to the mainstream of the college's operations. Large universities have the luxury of being able to hire full time staff to address accreditor requirements. Small colleges can't afford to do that.

There are steps that a college can be taking, in addition to assuring compliance with what the Commissions usually refer to as their 'standards of excellence.' Trustees would be well advised to at least know what the standards are, which are usually a dozen or so categories like 'mission,' 'financial stability,' 'student services,' 'governance,' and 'outcomes.' Of note are strategic planning and outcomes, both of which have become important evaluative measurements in recent times. Outcomes means results, like what happens to students after they graduate. Strategic Planning means what it says, although the assessment of the quality of the plan can vary depending on the knowledge of the evaluation team.

Trustees should realize that the Commissions are required to honor the stated purposes of the institution, usually as cited in its mission.

The Commission's charge is to assess whether the college is living up to its stated mission, including what the college says it is doing in its admissions recruiting materials. Overzealous admissions marketing materials can sometimes work against accreditation if promises are being made that are not being reflected in what is really happening at the college. To that end, Trustees should feel certain that the Mission Statement they have ratified is one that is feasible.

Each ten-year on-campus evaluation is preceded by a requirement for the college to submit a self-evaluation, according to the standards of excellence and other measurement criteria that are part of each region's accreditation requirements. The Commissions usually require that these self-studies be conducted by campus-wide committees comprised of all members of the community, including faculty, students, staff and trustees.

Trustees should probably know what the self-study is reporting to the accreditors before the report is submitted to the accreditors to at least insure that the promises being made are aligned with the policies established for the college by the Trustees. Sometimes, self-study members become advocates for their own ideologies that can redirect the college's priorities without Trustee knowledge.

While a task of the President, Trustees should at least know that the on-campus team members, as selected by the Commission, are presented to the President giving the

171

President an opportunity to comment on the team and request changes with cause. Many presidents are reluctant to challenge the team membership believing that such a challenge might adversely affect the college's favorable assessment. On the other hand, failure to remove an inappropriate member can have unforeseen consequences.

For example, virtually every evaluation team has a member with library expertise, as the library continues to be considered at the heart of all higher education institutions. A small college with a modest library can get cited for inadequacies by an evaluation-team representative who comes from a major public university with a library that is ten times larger. The President can request a change so that the library assessor comes from a college of comparable size.

Similarly, the chair of the team shouldn't be someone from an institutional background completely contrary to the college he or she is assessing. Usually, the Commission does try to make assignments that are comparable, but not always.

The faculty representatives are also worth scrutinizing. If your college has a non-unionized faculty, a faculty representative from a large public unionized faculty might not be the best evaluator. Presidents have to be careful not to challenge too many of the appointments, but should definitely question those whose backgrounds are from completely different worlds.

The best advice is to be sure that the college has someone who knows the accreditation process very well and knows how to line up all the requirements in a way that makes accreditation a routine without any potholes.

Then, if the Trustees are hearing very little about accreditation, that's because it isn't broken, and it doesn't need to be fixed.

Chapter 16

The Library Enigma

L ike faculty tenure, Trustees are faced with having to regard the Library as an untouchable sacred cow. At some point, major universities may take a lead that gives smaller colleges new ways to more efficiently provide library resources than is presently the case. How long such change will take is anyone's guess as the college library is a symbol of institutional intellectual commitment that dates back thousands of years to the great Alexandria library in Egypt that was a wonder of the world. To this day, universities often cite their academic stature in terms of the number of volumes in their library.

Accreditation agencies similarly have a number of measures, like the number of volumes, that they conclude correlate with academic excellence.

The technology renaissance of the past several decades has changed how everyone gets information, especially reference materials that change frequently and require regular update. The Internet has enable updated information to be available immediately making it virtually impossible for the traditional printed versions to keep pace. As often was the case in the past, academia has not been in the forefront of adapting to change and libraries often continue to hang on to outdated methods of maintaining information.

Back in the 1960's, when electronic calculators were first introduced, many university science, math and engineering professors refused to permit their students to use them. Rather, for quite an extended time after calculators had become readily available, these professors insisted that their students continue to use the slide rule for all calculations. Only slide rules were permitted in class and during examinations. It wasn't until slide rules were no longer being made or sold that faculty finally had to acquiesce and permit their students to use the much more accurate electronic calculators.

In the 1980's when personal computers were first introduced, many in academia had no interest and, to this day, some veteran faculty refuse to take advantage of what a laptop can do in the classroom. Similarly, some faculty remain opposed to books that are read on electronic devices.

Many photography professors spent most of the last decade resisting the advent of digital photography, insisting that their students continue to use film and chemical processing because, in their view, the quality of the photograph is so much better. Like slide rules, film and developing chemicals are becoming harder to purchase and are also more expensive. There will come a time when, like slide rules, all college photography courses are digital, but perhaps not until the alternatives of the past are extinct.

A recent visit to an urban law office illuminated the way in which books and libraries continue to be a symbol of scholarly excellence. The law firm featured, just beyond its reception area, a large conference room where clients met lawyers. The conference room contained floor-to-ceiling bookcases filled with leather-bound law journals.

When asked how often these law journals were used for case work, the managing partner of the law firm admitted that they were never used anymore. All legal research can be conducted much more readily, efficiently and thoroughly on the Internet. There, legal journals are updated on a daily basis where bound law journals are incomplete and thereby obsolete almost as soon as they are bound. Yet, the law office continues to subscribe to new editions of the leather bound issues in order to impress clients with their competence.

One can readily wonder how similar perceptions continue to influence the routine of the college library. Almost all academic disciplines have a professional society that, in turn, publishes professional journals containing articles on the discipline written by scholars. Often, these journals are a prime locale for the publishing requirement to which all professors are held, especially those yet to have earned tenure. Like law journals, many of these professional discipline journals published by organizations like the American Chemical Society or the American Sociological Association, to name just two of what must be hundreds of such groups, are expensive and, over time, take up a lot of space.

CBS's venerable 60 Minutes once visited a major American research university's on-campus library where virtually all the journals of all the disciplines were shelved, a requirement of the University's faculty. When asked who reads the journals, the head reference librarian admitted that virtually no one reads them. First, the research being published is largely of interest to fellow researchers, and rarely, if ever, to undergraduates. The librarian then noted that most scholars who are members of the associations have access to the articles on line and there is no need to have a hard copy in the library. But, having them in the library symbolizes the building's central role in the scholarship of the institution. Like the law library, the actual books are largely for show and not for any meaningful use.

My goodness, you're the first student to ask.
These journals aren't really needed by undergraduates,
but are required in order for us to be accredited.

Even smaller colleges can get caught up in spending blinding amounts of money, each year, on books that no one really needs or uses and, over time, take up space that could be better used. Some colleges have actually expanded their libraries in order to provide the necessary space for books.

While impossible to put into effect, monitoring book use in a library collection does at least seem like a good idea that could contribute to better resource allocation.

Some colleges and universities are addressing the library issue more directly and realistically than others. When Goucher College, in Maryland, built a new library a few years back, they designed a multi-purpose community center in the heart of the traffic patterns of the college. Called the Athenaeum, the building is not only a library, but also a coffee shop, a fitness center, a study room complex and a public forum for gatherings, receptions, large colloquia and, sometimes, performances. Reportedly, the use of the new multi-purpose library has eclipsed what had previously been a more remotely located library that was far from the most frequented building on campus.

The Harvard Graduate School of Education recently renovated its generations-old Gutman Library very dramatically turning the front entrance, main floor of the facility into a student lounge and café emulating, presumably, the modern version of a Barnes and Noble bookstore.

Many Boards do little to oversee what their college library is, or isn't, up to. They have no idea how much money, for instance, is being spent on books and journals that are rarely or never touched by human hands.

At some colleges, the library is required to acquire any book or journal that any professor requests. To what degree is that unmonitored activity occurring at your college? How much was spent on such acquisitions in recent years?

There may come a time, and some pundits say it is imminent, when paper books are as rare as slide rules and chemical film developing photography. When and if that happens, scholars and accreditors will have to look for ways other than the number of volumes, to assess the academic resources of a college.

Until then, Trustees should at least know where their library fits in the evolution and perhaps at least challenge the faculty and the administration to think ahead instead of resisting change until it becomes inevitable.

Chapter 17

Technology:
"Future Shock" has arrived

L ibraries are far from the only facet of higher education where technology is fundamentally changing every facet of our human existence at a more rapid pace than institutional willingness and financial ability seems receptive to accommodating. As observed in earlier chapters, colleges and universities are sometimes very resistant to any kind of change, especially ones that are technologically motivated. Resistance to abandoning bound-paper books is but one such phenomenon, as was the reluctance of science faculty to shelving slide rules when electric calculators were first introduced in the late 1960's. . .or when computerized financial spread sheets revolutionized accounting and business courses in the 1980's and when digital photography started to replace film and darkrooms in the 1990's.

Alvin Toffler's FUTURE SHOCK, first published in 1970, eloquently warned of the increasingly rapid changes that have been accelerating since the very beginning of time. In his book, he compared the entire lifetime of the Earth to a yardstick, then noting that bona fide humans have only been around during the last quarter inch of that yardstick. . .a time span of about 50,000 years. He went on to divide those years of human existence into 62-year life spans which resulted in little more than 800 consecutive lifetimes.

The first 650 of those 800 62-year lifetimes, he recounts, were spent in caves.

Only in the past 70 of those 800+ lifetimes has it been possible to communicate in any effective way from generation to generation.

For just six of those 800 lifetimes have any meaningful contingent of humankind been able to read printed words. For only five lifetimes has time been measured with precision. Electricity has only been available for the last three lifetimes.

Toffler's point was, simply enough, that time is moving at a logarithmic rate (meaning increasingly fast) which is particularly being borne out when it comes to way in which technological progress is. . . pardon the redundancy . . .progressing.

The blurring rate of this progress is arguably making much of higher education's traditional ways of teaching more obsolete than many academicians wish to recognize.

The fact is that today's college student is rapidly becoming someone who never existed in the twentieth century. They have never 'dialed' a phone number. They have never 'taped' a television program. The Beatles performance on the Ed Sullivan Show, now nearly a half century ago, is equivalent to college students in the early 60's reflecting back on a pre-WWI firsts like George Bernard Shaw's first production of Pygmalion in London and Henry Ford's first automobile assembly line being introduced.

Any professor over 50 graduated from college having never used a personal computer.

There is no getting away from the reality that technology is here to stay and continues to revolutionize just

183

about every facet of life, including teaching and learning. As any Trustee already knows, the costs associated with keeping up with, much less being in the forefront of, educational technology is financially overwhelming and is up there with insurance costs and employee benefits as being straws that collectively are breaking the camel's back, especially the backs of smaller, enrollment-revenue dependent camels.

Any higher education institution wishing to attract and enroll good students will not succeed if they get too far behind in basic technology resources.

Basic,' today, includes a completely wireless campus. There shouldn't be a place anywhere on campus where students cannot connect to the Internet with the laptops and iPad-type devices, including all classrooms and, most importantly in many ways, their rooms. Also important is that the band is large enough to accommodate hundreds or thousands of students downloading and streaming simultaneously

Today's college students have been computer-literate since birth and aren't going to change or otherwise adapt to college standards that are not keeping up.

One area where many small colleges fall short is in administrative technology, including systems that enable immediate message communication to all students and to all student families, course registration and other such routine services. Alumni and related fund-raising and development communications should, by now, also be completely connected to the technological vehicles that are now commonplace.

Many small colleges have done little to upgrade their classrooms, often because they know that their veteran faculty won't. . .*don't know how to*. . .use the technology. And, too many, because they don't know how, reject the relevance of such technology. Like electronic calculators and digital cameras, teaching technology is being viewed by many veteran faculty as a negative trend in education that they must condemn in order to preserve the classic values of pedagogy. Too often, such 'ideological' arguments are more because those same faculty are at a point in their careers where they refuse to divert from the teaching models they have comfortably employed for decades.

There is probably not a lot Trustees at smaller colleges can do to accelerate the process of change in teaching methods and probably should let nature take its course, unless there is clear evidence that the lack of change is impairing enrollment health. Instead, smaller colleges will have to await national trends that have been adopted by the most highly regarded universities and colleges. As the Ivies, among others, appear to be moving rather aggressively into the worlds of potentially better mousetraps, perhaps smaller colleges won't have to wait that long to join in.

Without question, though, Trustees should be vigilant to insure that the college's technological resources are at least up to the standard of full accessibility for student use throughout the campus. If possible, one of the most valuable Trustee additions would be a technology industry mogul.

Students are often light years ahead of their college professors in their computer wherewithal and it might be interesting to inquire whether there is a way in which students can critique the 'computer literacy' of the institution and cite those areas that are wanting.

This could be a useful early warning system that permits Trustees to understand the comfort level of students with respect to the college's available resources. Falling too far behind could be a reason for students to transfer elsewhere.

Chapter 18

Is On-Line Learning "The" Future?

There likely isn't a Trustee who hasn't been hearing that their college should be looking into the 'next big thing:' namely, on-line learning. Or, as some believe, it is the current big thing. Over the past decade or two, there has been an international surge in on-line courses and many small colleges have attempted to be leaders in offering such course-work, presumably hoping that they can find a meaningful revenue stream to offset tuition revenues from full time students.

More recently, even the Ivy League universities have begun to experiment with on-line course offerings thereby making it very unlikely that any small, financially-limited college can now enter the online market with any hopes of making the kind of money that offsets the costs of a stand-alone enterprise.

MOOC , meaning 'massively open online courses,' typically free, is the prevailing buzz word for a phenomenon that is being characterized as the wave of the future.

So much so that even Harvard and MIT have formed a non-profit partnership they are calling edX which offers free online courses taught at both universities. Stanford, Princeton, and the Universities of Pennsylvania and Michigan have formed another more commercial venture called Coursera. The usage statistics are impressive. Coursera recently reported that their usage has grown to nearly 2.5 million students taking their on-line courses out of nearly three-dozen universities, including internationally. Harvard-MIT's edX first course offering reportedly drew over 150,000 students.

The up-front investment and expertise in this 'next big thing' exceeds what most small, tuition-revenue-dependent colleges can possibly hope to find within their existing infrastructure and budget. And, any such college hoping to find a cornucopia of new revenues from such ventures will likely go broke long before they realize their first dollar.

If, however, there is existing faculty expertise motivated to develop small, pilot programs unique to the college, that probably shouldn't be discouraged.

Nevertheless , any hope that on-line learning is a short-term revenue silver bullet, offsetting revenue shortages being experienced by excessive discounting and enrollment declines, seems likely to end up disappointing.

While times may now be different than just a decade ago, heeding the failures of the past would recall a 2001 venture called Fathom, that was launched by Columbia University partnering with the Universities of Chicago and Michigan. After major financial setbacks, it closed down just two years later as did a Yale, Princeton and Stanford venture, AllLearn, that closed down in 2006.

That said, on line learning appears here to stay. The big question, perhaps, is when it will start making money and who will be making that money.

At least one major university in the East, for instance, appears to be very proud of its on-line MBA degree. While this highly regarded urban university insists that it is their MBA, the on-line aspect of it is subcontracted to a private corporation, of which there are now seven or eight such companies in the forefront of a booming field. The company designed the technology and fundamentally runs the on-line component. The university, as a result, reportedly receives only 15% of the revenues realized. While that has resulted in at least $2 million in revenues for the University that they arguably might not have otherwise realized, it is little more than the equivalent tuition revenues that would have been received from several dozen on-campus MBA students where 100% of the revenues were realized by the University.

Another question, yet unanswered, that universities subcontracting to on-line companies have to wonder about, is whether the cache of their degree offerings will be adversely affected, in the long run, because their diploma is being awarded to students completing on-line coursework administered by a corporate subcontractor that takes 85% of the revenue.

The arrangement is reminiscent of branding that has for ages been subcontracted in business products. The French fashion designer, Pierre Cardin, is an interesting case to heed. In the 1950's, Cardin was at the top of the profession and his fashion wear was the Harvard of the industry. The Cardin name had such universal appeal that hundreds of manufacturers bought the Cardin name for their products which eventually extended to low-priced men's tie tacks and cufflinks to baby toys. Cardin's name was everywhere, including in the lowest end of retailing chains.

For at least a decade or more, Pierre Cardin made a fortune in royalties from all the products being sold with his name. While he insisted that he carefully monitored the quality of the products using his name, the low price and ubiquitous availability eventually took all prestige and cache away from the quality of the Pierre Cardin brand name which no longer had a Harvard 'ring' to it.

Whether anything comparable happens to the relative stature of university degrees remains to be seen and, to that end, **WHAT COLLEGE TRUSTEES NEED TO KNOW** is limited, from the vantage point of this book, to strongly advising that Trustees watch this trend carefully and be open to meaningful prospects while being wary of the potential potholes.

There are a lot of companies that have been formed to design and manage on-line course offerings for colleges. Which ones will prevail and make their clients money remains to be seen and is very difficult to predict.

Be mindful that anyone who had invested $10,000 in Microsoft stock when it was initially offered in 1986 would now have over $3 million in value a quarter century later. Anyone who had bought $10,000 of Apple stock just a decade ago would now have more than a half million dollars. But, anyone who had bought $10,000 shares of Cisco Systems stock just 13 years ago when it surpassed Microsoft as the most valuable company in the world, would now have less than $3,000. When dealing with the 'next big thing,' there is invariably a lot of people getting into the act and not all will be winners.

And, if all the Ivies, along with other major name-brand universities throughout the country, continue to seek no revenue for their on-line courses, it is hard to fathom the prospect that on-line students will forgo the free Ivy League courses and instead pay for a course from a small, private college. For now, there is no course credit and certainly no Harvard degree being offered for students who take their courses on line.

But, some smaller colleges are reportedly already gearing up to grant course credit for on-line students taking the free Harvard courses. Presumably, they will charge a modest fee for granting that credit, but they will also be granting a modest degree as compared to Harvard credit.

Since these smaller colleges will be spending nothing on instruction, the cost of granting credit for free Harvard courses that Harvard is not awarding credit for will presumable be less than the fee charged for smaller college credit, thereby giving them a revenue stream that could grow.

Should free on-line courses go global, there could be billions of students eventually taking free courses which would make even a $1 course credit fee add up to a blinding amount of money.

So, stay tuned . . . and in tune.

Chapter 19

Fund Raising

In recent decades, fund raising has taken center stage in higher education and is often cited as the single-most important task of the President and the Board. . .especially the President. It is not unusual to see fund raising cited in presidential search announcements as the primary responsibility of the next president who should be prepared to be 'on the road' fundraising as much as 50% of the time.

There are perhaps many college presidencies where the college is operating so well that the chief executive is rarely needed for on-campus routines and can therefore be 'on the road' up to half the time. Most of the colleges for which this book has been written are not among those prosperous and flourishing institutions not needing presidential oversight.

Any college discounting tuition more than 40% needs a substantial on-campus presidential presence to re-tool the institution so it is generating the necessary resources to serve students at a level they have a right to expect.

Unfortunately, any school struggling with enrollment revenue and operating costs is inclined to dream about how all their problems would be solved if they only had an endowment. . .thereby sending off their president to find the pot of gold at the end of the rainbow instead of addressing operating fundamentals.

Every time a $50 million, $100 million (or even more) gift to a university or college is announced, presidents and fund raising vice presidents throughout higher education are swamped with emails and telephone calls, including from Trustees, asking when a gift like that is going to be given to their particular college. Like the national lottery, everyone dreams of such a windfall although few, very few, will actually ever realize such a miracle. But, that cold water doesn't seem to stop anyone from aspiring and believing it can happen to them too. As the lottery advertisements declare. . .*Hey, you never know.*

Well, in fact, the realities are pretty sobering. While it seems like major multi-million dollar gifts happen frequently in higher education, the actual number of occurrences, especially for smaller colleges, is miniscule given the number of colleges and universities in the USA.

Over the past 20 years or so, about 135 gifts of $100 million or more have been realized in higher education.

On average, that is about seven such gifts each year. What is most sobering, though, is that over 60, nearly half, of those gifts have all gone to fewer than twenty of the top universities that comprise the Ivy League, MIT, NYU, Stanford, UCal, USC and UTexas. The other half have also gone to major national colleges and universities.

Fewer than 12 of those 135 gifts were realized by the 1,500 smaller, tuition-dependent institutions for which this book has been written. That is about one in 1,500 every other year for the past 20 years.

The story doesn't change all that much when looking at gifts between $50 million and $100 million. About 160 such gifts have been cited over the past 20 years and about 15 such gifts, again less than 10%, went to smaller tuition dependent institutions.

Of course, these 300 mega-gifts don't rule out how welcome even one or two million dollar gifts can be to smaller colleges. However, the 'smell the coffee' fact remains that most smaller colleges will not realize gifts large enough to meaningfully change the tuition-revenue dependency that they are almost certain to face indefinitely. Yet, many such institutions routinely focus their giving priorities on building an endowment first and foremost, perhaps because presidential careers, when they come to an end, are often too heavily measured by the size of endowment growth during their tenure.

Particularly in today's low-interest rate economy, even large endowments don't contribute a meaningful amount to annual operating revenues.

A $100 million endowment will contribute only one or two million dollars annually which would still keep most small colleges over 90% tuition dependent. By comparison, an increase of fewer than 75 additional full-paying students generates the same amount of annual revenue as a $100 million endowment realizes in spendable interest income. Finding 75 additional paying students is arguably a more

prudent expectation than finding $100 million in endowment giving.

The role of major multi-million dollar gifts in any ambitious fund raising aspiration must also be understood. Any president and Board deciding to set, say, a $50 million goal has to realize that most of that money will have to come from a relatively small number of major donors.

$50 million, in $1,000 gifts, will require 50,000 such individual donations. That just isn't going to happen at smaller colleges and universities. Even at the $10,000 level, 5,000 such gifts are needed, which is also very unlikely.

Another old tenet of fund raising rings true. . .namely, that **90% of any fund raising goal will come from 5% of the donors**, thereby requiring, for $50 million, at least four or five gifts in excess of $5 million, or two to three in the $10 million range. No ambitious campaign should be launched without a realistic sense of likely sources for such major gifts.

Nevertheless, tuition-dependent colleges are revenue-hungry and pursue the elusive

brass ring of major gifts in ways that can sometimes defy reality.

These same colleges sometimes build disproportionately large fund-raising organizations often modeled after major university fund raising operations. Development offices can include departments for annual giving, alumni reunion giving, corporate giving, foundation giving, planned giving, major giving, capital campaign giving, and more. Each of these offices is then staffed with directors, secretaries and support personnel, all of which require operating budgets for technology, postage, publications, travel, entertainment and events. Big dollars can add up pretty quickly to an amount that can come close to exceeding the amount of money raised. When that happens, fund raising personnel will typically contend that giving is not a one-year undertaking. . .that processes are being put in place for results that may take years to be realized. When, years later, nothing really improves, these same personnel move on to other worlds where they start all over again with a similar time line for their results.

Trustees and presidents need to critically assess the costs vs. the outcomes. . .and, perhaps in fairness to the longitudinal factors associated with cultivating donors, should conduct such assessments over a multi-year span of time. Smaller colleges and universities not untypically realize modest fund raising outcomes as compared to major national colleges and universities. One-to-two million dollars a year in unrestricted giving is not an unrealistic expectation for schools with 2500 students or fewer. Some of these same schools, however, have development operating budgets that approach and sometimes exceed one million dollars a year resulting, in some cases, in an outcome where most everything donated ends up doing little more than paying for the costs of soliciting it and sometimes not even that.

Charities other than higher education tend to be more carefully scrutinized by government agencies for the ratio of costs vs. funds donated.

Typically, no more than 25% of giving is considered an acceptable level of fund raising expenditure. When more than 25% is spent on administrative costs unrelated to the purpose of the charity, such institutions face the prospect of losing their tax-exempt status. Likewise, donors to colleges and universities, even small donors, would be pretty alarmed were they to learn that 85% of their gift paid for the staff in the annual giving office.

Trustees would be well advised to question the value of any Development function that isn't annually realizing four-times its operating costs.

This is especially relevant to annual giving, corporate and foundation relations. Small colleges should question the advisability of even having a corporate and foundation relations office. Most corporations and foundations are not inclined to give to smaller colleges unless a very senior officer is an alumnus/a. Those few institutions that might be prospective donors can be handled directly by the chief development officer and the president, as can the cultivation of major donors, thereby negating the need for a major gifts officer. If there is a planned giving office, that function too should be closing on irrevocable trusts and the like at a rate that approaches four times the costs of the function. . .even though such gifts are not realized until after the donor dies, because they can be booked as an asset.

Trustees should also be looking carefully at what is, and isn't, being cited as a cost of fund raising. Unless alumni are paying a membership fee to cover the costs of an alumni office, which is rarely the case, all alumni staffing and operating costs should be included in the costs of fund raising and, hopefully, are being underwritten by four times their cost in alumni annual giving.

Sometimes, publications, mailings, telephones and other costs of fundraising are in centralized administrative accounts and therefore not incorporated into the development operating budget. Similarly, the costs of special events hosted by the President for donor prospects are in the President's Office budget rather than the development office. Even office costs and capital acquisitions should be counted into the costs of fundraising.

At tuition-dependent colleges, Trustees need to remind themselves that whenever alumni and fund-raising costs exceed what is being raised, the difference is being paid by currently enrolled students and their families and thereby contributing to the trillion dollar debt they have already accrued. Therefore, any fund raising program that is spending more than it is realizing should be considered, in every way, unacceptable.

As there are many books dedicated to fundraising strategies, not to mention a professional newspaper, *The Chronicle of Philanthropy*, this book won't dwell on the fundamentals.

Presidents and Trustees should all read a marvelous book titled **FUND RAISING REALITIES EVERY BOARD MEMBER MUST FACE** by David Lansdowne. Cited as a 'one hour' read, this very efficiently written manual features two-to-three page chapters that do indeed qualify as information that every Trustee should know. The book has been in print for well over a decade.

Without stealing Lansdowne's thunder, one of the most important reminders cited in the book is that truly successful fundraising has to involve the president and the Trustees in a central and collaborative way. While this is true throughout higher education, regardless of institutional size and stature, it is particularly essential for smaller colleges lacking national top shelf brand name recognition.

Even though most presidential search announcements cite fundraising as a top priority for candidates, presidential decisions often appear relatively void of that demonstrated expertise. More about that in another chapter. Presidents who don't like fund raising often compensate by building large, and expensive, fund raising organizations to which that responsibility can be, and too typically is, delegated. Trustees have also been known to dislike and avoid involvement in fund raising, thereby supporting the presidential delegation of fund raising. As any competent fund-raising executive will be quick to affirm. . .

The likelihood of major fund raising outcomes being realized by a college development office is highly unlikely without significant Presidential and Trustee involvement, especially at smaller colleges.

Few, if any, major donors are going to decide to donate millions of their dollars to an institution where they don't feel that they know the president, and, for that matter, the Board leadership. To the contrary, **successful major donor relationships require long and on-going cultivation that the president and board cannot delegate. Any president not 'willing and able' to do that kind of work shouldn't be the president.**

Trustees and presidents need to be asking themselves what they are prepared to do to make a meaningful improvement in the tuition-dependency of the institution. If they are committed to building a substantial endowment that will have a relieving impact on tuition dependence, they have to realize that the endeavor will likely take decades and maybe even generations.

One million dollars buys a professor just a chair?
I remember when that kind of money
would get my name on a college building !!!

Multi-million dollar gifts aren't realized quickly and rarely come from sources that have not experienced a long relationship with the college, especially at smaller institutions that lack the world stature of the Ivy League, Stanford, MIT and other such gold standard universities.

The Peddie School in New Jersey is a good example of the patience sometimes necessary to realize a $100 million gift. Publishing legend Walter Annenberg was a 1927 graduate of the Peddie School. For decades thereafter, the Peddie School cultivated their billionaire alumnus as he endowed schools of communication at the University of Pennsylvania and Syracuse University. Then, in 1993, nearly 70 years after his graduation, Annenberg finally made a $100 million gift.

Henry Rowan's $100 million gift to Glassboro State University, made twenty years ago in 1993, and which resulted in an institutional name-change to Rowan University, is another example of a 'courtship' that took decades.

Among the many tenets of fund raising is that few major gifts, if any, come from 'proposing marriage on the first date.' Presidents and Trustees have to be prepared for a long courtship that does not convey a sense that their interest in any prospective donor is largely because they are a prospective donor.

**College presidents today must like being
with people and need to have the talent to
convey an infectious enthusiasm about the
college while also being a great listener;
someone who has the talent to appear genuinely
interested in the donors being courted. . .or,
even better, IS genuinely interested.**

Presidents and Trustees committed to a major fund
raising outcome that will build a substantial endowment need
to focus on major donor prospects that they are prepared to
cultivate for years, maybe decades while also realizing that
most such gifts are likely to be realized as bequests.

**Another long standing tenet of major
giving is that such donors, while living, are most
drawn to seeing the impact of their donation,
thereby making what is colloquially called
'bricks and mortar' a much more seductive
giving target than endowment.**

More often than not, major endowment gifts come
from bequests, meaning, needless to say, that the donor
must first die. This sobering reality has made planned
giving a very important part of major giving when targeted
for endowments. Planned giving has become even more

attractive in today's low interest rate environment when traditional conservative investments, like long term CDs, no longer pay very much.

Many colleges and universities have successfully built a long term pipeline of future major contributions to endowment through the establishment of irrevocable trusts made by major donors who receive a much higher annual rate of return established by the college, while also enjoying the tax deductions of having made a major donation. This is one area where a very seasoned development officer can generate results that far exceed the program's cost, including high salaries. Such professionals can present themselves, somewhat accurately, as investment counselors. . .not just donation solicitors.

People with the capacity to give multi-million dollar gifts will all acknowledge that their wealth is being sought by more worthy causes than they could possibly underwrite in major ways. Colleges and universities, especially those that are alma maters to such wealthy sources, have a great advantage as there is something about one's college days and one's youth that gains in importance and value as mortality becomes a sobering reality. But, while alma maters have a strong advantage, major donors who finally commit to multi-million dollar gifts will almost always acknowledge that they made the commitment not only because they cared about their alma mater, but they felt a continuing relationship due to the way in which the President and the Trustees had folded them into the heart of the institution.

IF YOU'RE GIVIN'
WHEN YOU'RE LIVIN',
YOU'RE KNOWIN'
WHERE IT'S GOIN'

While endowment-*itis* is a prevailing obsession among colleges and universities, Trustees should heed the fact that major donations are easier to realize when the donor can see where the donation is going.

What donors can most readily see are improvements to the campus. Revenue-dependent colleges and universities do have to face the reality that they are an expensive consumer product in a marketplace overloaded with comparable expensive consumer products.

Enrollment recruiting experts have long cited the campus visit, and the inspection of the campus, to be the single-most important factor that most families employ when making a college decision. Colleges without a fully-equipped campus, especially technologically and living conditions, may be best advised to focus their major fundraising efforts on gifts that are invested, not in endowment, but in helping the college succeed in that 'single-most important' influence.

Admissions recruiting marketing campaigns almost all cite institutional excellence in virtually all dimensions.

Many colleges don't live up to that characterization during the first visit. If you are selling a Lexus-priced product, it better have power steering, air conditioning and leather upholstery. In college terms, that might translate to facilities like an expansive fitness center, full-service computer technology, a performing arts center and reasonably private bathrooms in the residence halls.

This is where fund raising can be a silver bullet.

Major donors can most readily get excited about adding a facility that strengthens the competitive position of an institution. Those same major donors are much harder to persuade when asked to make a comparably large donation to endowment.

A college generating 'wows' during campus visits can draw hundreds of new students that otherwise might never even apply. Two hundred additional students can net an additional $7 million annually. A $300 million endowment would probably be required to generate as much.

No one would argue that it would be ideal to have both 'bricks and mortar' major gifts and endowment, but any institution lacking the quality facilities, sought by families financially able to pay private college tuition rates, is shooting itself in the foot by focusing 'first and foremost' on endowment while concurrently leaving the campus under-resourced, or worse, in disrepair. In that respect, a president overseeing an institution that is not successfully recruiting and retaining paying students shouldn't be 'on the road' 50% of the time.

Chapter 20

Board Composition

Volumes have already been written about Boards of Trustees and their role in overseeing colleges and universities. Much of that information has been published in a library of books and articles available from the Association of Governing Boards (AGB). Rather than recount much of what is already out there, here are just a few items, including some red flags, that Boards of smaller, enrollment-revenue dependent institutions should consider and measure their own Board organization against.

While there is no universally agreed upon rule for Board size, it does sometimes seem that there is an inverse correlation between the size of the Board and the size of the institution. Smaller colleges too often assemble massive Boards that far exceed what is necessary and, more importantly, practical. By comparison, the governing board of Harvard University's, called the Corporation, has been an assemblage of fewer than a dozen and only now is in the process of expanding its ranks to a new high of 13 members.

Bigger isn't always better

While there may not be an ultimate, scientifically-proven ideal size, many management textbooks cite the dysfunctions that intensify when decision-making bodies grow larger than twenty or so participants. Some contend that the most effective groups don't exceed a dozen. The reason for such theories is largely based on the potential for meaningful interaction that diminishes in oversized groups.

Faculty would be among the first to contend that student interaction and participation in classroom dynamics is greatly subdued when the class size exceeds 20 students. Larger groups become audiences instead of participants.

Any Board of Trustees that becomes too large subjects itself to the same problems that students in large classes experience. They are likely to find themselves not really engaging all that much, but rather listening to reports and approving motions.

Quality vs. quantity applies to Boards of Trustees in the same way it applies to the size of the applicant pool, as covered earlier in this book.

An argument frequently made on behalf of a large Board is the advantage of optimizing the number of people (especially people of power, access and financial wherewithal) in the life blood of the college. Quite correctly, Development professionals will contend that major donations will most usually come from those people who feel an integral part of the institution. Therefore, those same fundraisers would advocate: the larger the Board, the larger the potential prospective donors list.

While Boards probably should be heavily populated with the College's most promising major donors, not all such donors want to bear the responsibilities, fiscally and legally, that go with Board membership. A good alternative to overly large Boards is to establish an array of Advisory Committees that meet perhaps no more frequently than once a year.

In addition to Harvard's baker's dozen "Corporation," the University has many other non-governing boards including a Board of Overseers along with Visiting Committees for each of the University's graduate schools.

These secondary boards may be populated with prospective major donors, but ones who also expertise and a personal interest in the specific area of the University which their non-governing Board is given a role in advising. During their infrequent visits, such Boards are fully briefed on what has been transpiring since their last visit and are invited to critique and provide counsel. These non-governing boards also include sub-groups of the college, like faculty and students. However, these groups are not involved in the fiscal matters of the institution, nor in setting policy.

In addition to oversized Boards, populating the Trustees with members who represent constituencies can pose serious problems when Boards face having to make tough decisions aimed at averting crises. All Board members should be able to say that their role is to pursue what is in the best interests of the entire college without a bias for a particular subgroup or ideology. If any Board members are selected to represent, say, the faculty, or the student body, or a founding religion, they are advocate on behalf of their constituency which can sometimes be contrary to what is in the best interests of the institution as seen by the majority of those involved and affected.

Adversities of meeting too frequently

As there is no universally agreed-upon tenet for Board size, there also seems to be a wide-array of views with respect to how often Trustees should meet. Some

Boards meet monthly which most institutions would probably, and rightly, conclude is too frequent. Boards are of greatest value to the college when they are populated by successful and powerful people; people who not only bring expertise, but also can enable access. Access to resources. Access to arenas of stature and visibility. Access to other successful and powerful people. Access to donors and other sources of philanthropy.

The more successful and powerful a person is, the more demands are being placed on his or her time. Such people are not going to be able to set aside several days a month to attend Trustee meetings. At the same time, they are only going to become committed to their Board membership if they feel that their time is being well used.

To that end, it is probably in the best interests of the college to schedule no more than three meetings a year and perhaps as few as two in locations that pose lengthy travel times from the major urban centers of the US. In such cases, perhaps the best two times for annual Board meetings are immediately before or after the Homecoming weekend in the fall, and similarly before or after Commencement in the spring. That way Trustees also get to experience particularly uplifting events in the College's annual calendar that can add immensely to their pride in and commitment to the institution. Needless to say, such scheduling poses an enormous burden on senior personnel who are probably overtaxed when just addressing one of the events, but the payoffs can make the investment worth the effort.

Two meetings a year is too infrequent, of course, for colleges facing serious financial problems that, in turn, create problems throughout the college. Probably the best way to be more vigilant is to have a core Executive Committee that can convene whenever needed and, if necessary, as frequently as monthly, keeping the full Board apprised of their interim activities.

The technology breakthroughs of the past decade or two have made it much easier for Boards to meet without all having to be in the same place at the same time. All colleges, and especially those in remote locales, should invest in a conference room with large flat screens along with a conference table that can permit each attendee to participate via audio-visual hookups like SKYPE. That enables even the busiest Trustees to participate as frequently as monthly without having to set aside days in travel time to the campus.

Board Committee Red Flags

The more Trustees a college has, the more they have to find ways to keep everyone engaged beyond the actual full Board meetings. All Boards have committees. The most usual ones are Executive, Finance, Academic and Development. The larger the Board, the more committees

217

. . . or so it seems to be. Other frequently established committees can include athletics, student life, community relations, buildings and grounds, and, even public relations.

The narrower the role of the committee, the more likely it is going to engage in micro-management activities that subjugate the authority of the chief executive officer.

At the more trivial level, some buildings and grounds committees take over decisions like what colors walls should be painted, what style of furniture should be purchased and what brand of computer should be purchased.

At the more crippling level, some Finance and Academic Board committees can become a powerful advocacy group for subordinates of the chief executive officer in ways that can enable those subordinates to circumvent the president to whom they should report with Trustee support.

More than one chief financial officer (CFO) has been known to declare that he/she reports to the Board Finance Committee and _not_ to the President. When a college president is hired whose background is largely academic, which is frequently the case when a Provost becomes President, the CFO can quickly ascertain that the President knows little about financial management. Even where this may well be the case, management chaos can be the result of a CFO and Board Finance Committee taking over the financial control of the College. All constituencies within the college begin to realize that the only way in which they are going to get the resources they need to operate is to make their case to the CFO who will, in turn, take that advocacy to the Board Finance Committee. By the time the budget gets to the President or the Full Board, the deliberations are largely over and have largely circumvented the President. When that happens, the President loses authority in just about every meaningful way.

If a Board is going to hold a chief executive accountable for institutional outcomes, the Board has to be careful not to take authority away from him/her by establishing committees that exceed their role as overseers and instead become management decision making entities.

As the CFO has been known to do with the Board Finance Committee, Provosts are often just as culpable in their dealings with the Academic Affairs Committee. As with all Board committees, the senior staff liaison for each committee is the executive, logically enough, with responsibility for the area. As rational as that relationship seems, the very structure can work against the smooth running of the management infrastructure of the college if the Board committees assert too much decision making advocacy. Provosts have been known to use the Academic Affairs Committee as a lobbying entity within the Board of Trustees in order to minimize presidential and Trustee intervention in the academic program and to insulate the academic programs from fiscal realities.

Academic Committees of Boards are typically comprised of those Trustees who are not executives, financiers, entrepreneurs and the like, all of whom usually seek membership on the Board Executive or Finance committees. The Academic Committee members will themselves be academics or others who are seen as more interested in the qualitative rather than the quantitative. Boards can err in allowing this sort of self-selection to take place as they will staff the Academic Committee with personnel who are not looking at the practical side of instruction which, when not monitored, can greatly burden the costs of a small college as explained in earlier chapters.

To prevent such problems, Board chairs should avoid staffing committees in too homogenous a way. Academic Affairs committees, for example, should include one or two Trustees who have executive management and fiscal backgrounds. That way, someone on the Committee can ask some of the quantitative questions associated, for example, with the advisability of starting a new academic major.

Equally important, all Board committees should be properly briefed in what they are there to do. First and foremost, they should not become review boards for budgetary needs being sought by the staff liaison to the Committee. Nor, should they in any way conduct themselves in a manner that encourages the staff liaison to take all his/her problems, along with wish lists, to their Board Committee thereby seeking advocacy for differences of opinion that exists between the liaison and the President. Board committees shouldn't emulate grandparents succumbing to the demands of their children's children.

Under no circumstances should the Finance Committee take on the role of hearing budget requests from college subgroups, including the CFO. Only those budget proposals approved by the President, that presumably were the culmination of a management decision making process, should be on the Finance Committee agenda. If the CFO is taking an independent agenda to the Finance Committee that is contrary to the chief executive or, worse, not known to the chief executive, then the Trustees are making a bad situation worse.

In a nutshell, all Trustees need to respect the very important requirement that, **officially, the Board must speak with one voice.**

For centuries, if not from the beginning of mankind, Machiavelli's revelations in The Prince are at the core of human nature when it comes to influence and power. A Board divided, or one where Trustees take it upon themselves to be independent advocates, and to form coalitions within the college, will contribute more to chaos than to order and progress. Advocacy groups will divide and conquer, taking advantage of the opportunity to build their own coalitions within the Board. The president's authority will be severely impaired as will the full Board's ability to find common ground that can move the College forward.

Chapter 21

The Presidential Search

Probably the most important responsibility of a Board of Trustees is the hiring, assessing and, when necessary, firing of the chief executive **officer**. While Trustees still play the dominant role in presidential assessment and termination, much of the selection process has been, perhaps involuntarily, turned over to a wider array of participants. In recent decades, the presidential hiring process has evolved into an expensive and time-consuming undertaking called, more often than not, the 'national search.' Presumably, so goes conventional wisdom,

223

the only way in which an institution can be assured they
have located and hired the best president is to certify that
they have conducted a search that has involved everyone
from everywhere and has turned over every rock in the
universe doing so.

Maybe it is the for-profit executive search firms that
have, over time, successfully persuaded the higher education
community that *only they* can conduct such a complex and
exhaustive search process, thereby guaranteeing an
optimum outcome. Needless to say, this has spawned dozens
of search firms specializing in presidential searches. Today,
rare is the presidential search that has not been delegated,
at considerable and often crippling expense, to one of these
search firms.

**Although Trustees will typically insist that
theirs is the final decision, the fact is that many
search processes leave little to decide when it
comes down to the final Board vote.**

The institutional community, especially the faculty,
has carved out a role for itself that almost insures that no
presidential candidate they don't like will have a chance.

The process has become so complex that it is
fundamentally impossible to complete the ordeal in less than
a year. And, each step along the way is expensive while

much of the undertaking is of questionable necessity and value.

First, the search firm must be selected. All aspiring firms will present a list of former clients that report they were happy with the outcome. Of course, no institution is going to publicly admit that they weren't happy with the outcome as it would cast a shadow on their decision and on the credibility of the president they chose. Searches that have been failures are not acknowledged by the search firms, and certainly not by the institutional clients.

One such failure occurred a few years back at a small, relatively well regarded, undergraduate college that hired one of the national search firms. The search firm reportedly showcased a graduate school dean from a prestigious national, public university. Largely because of the stature of that prestigious university, the dean was hired even though he/she had no experience with undergraduates or at small, independent colleges. Well, the new president was quickly discovered to be the wrong fit in almost every essential way. His/her departure was cited as having nothing to do with performance. To save face, he/she announced, as per usual, that he/she was moving on to new challenges. Another search was conducted. An additional year was lost.

Another very comparable search was conducted at a small college in the East. Once again, a provost from a prominent research university was selected. He/she also had no prior experience at undergraduate, residential colleges and was gone shortly after only a year on the job.

A not-infrequent mistake made in searches is to be drawn to the prestigious brand name of the candidate's current job or prior positions, rather than hands-on and successful leadership experience at a comparable institution.

Trustees should also be pondering what kind of background is best suited for a college presidency.

More often than not, Provosts (or chief academic officers) are considered to be the best suited candidates and some have indeed become exemplary presidents.

At the same time, Trustees should be reminded that. . .

The job of President, especially at smaller, tuition-dependent undergraduate colleges, is very different than the responsibilities of a Provost.

A Provost is the chief academic officer spending virtually all of his/her time concerned about the faculty and about instruction/curriculum. On the one hand, what is more important or central to a University than the quality of the academic program? Probably nothing is more important. On the other hand . . .

Most of what a President is called upon to do emphasizes finance, marketing, external relations, fund raising and other broader responsibilities often of little relevance to anything that a Provost had been doing. . . or, even, likes to do.

Would a veteran airplane pilot, for instance, make the best president of an airline company? Would a brain surgeon make the best CEO of a hospital?

Doctors and pilots may, and probably would, answer yes to that question. But, really?

While the faculty members of a presidential search committee will typically be most drawn to candidates with strong backgrounds as scholars, researchers, and professors. . . .ergo, Provosts. . .Trustees need to be certain that such favored candidates can be as effective in the areas where they have had little to no experience. That is a tall order that many Provosts can't fill.

Probably the best candidates for presidential openings are those who have been a president elsewhere and have proven they can do the job. However, the year-long, egalitarian process overseen by search firms and involving dozens of search committee members from within the institution make it almost impossible for a sitting president to participate as a candidate in these highly visible processes.

Contrary to assurances of confidentiality, there is little likelihood of confidentiality in the presidential search firm processes typical of the national search firm model. More recently, Internet domains like Facebook and blogs have all but assured that all candidates for a college presidency will be revealed and their identities will be widely disseminated.

Any college president who becomes known at his/her institution as being an applicant/ candidate for another presidency elsewhere may just as well be revealed as cheating on a spouse, as far as their current institution, seeing itself married to its president, will be concerned.

Just as bad, if not worse, is _not_ being selected for the job after having applied for it. That can bring into question whether he/she should continue as President wherever they are presently employed if they are not seen as worthy elsewhere, and are looking to move on thereby reflecting their lack of commitment to their existing presidency.

The Provost, on the other hand, can explain that he/she is looking at a position that is a career step upward. Somehow, that isn't cheating or otherwise symbolizing a betrayal of loyalty to their current institution.

Thus, many of the best candidates, who would love to be in the position, never come forward for consideration and likely never will.

The risk is too high for the uncertain probability of outcome.

The fact is that the current search firm process, contrary to conventional wisdom, really doesn't assure that the best qualified candidate will be selected.

Another problem interfering with optimal outcome is that there are just too many special interests that can prevail and thereby eliminate otherwise ideal candidates. Such biases can, and often do, include too many. . .

Faculty who demand extensive past
teaching and research scholarship.

Religious advocates at many colleges,
especially in the East, whose founding
roots emanate from a specific church.

Members steadfastly committed
to a female or minority appointment.

While all of the above criteria certainly shouldn't
deter favorable consideration and appointment, none should
be a prerequisite for level-playing ground consideration.

**Boards of Trustees should assess whether
stepping into the obligatory, time-consuming
and expensive, national search firm process is
indeed in the best interest of the institution.**

The Trustees will likely have to assemble a search
committee comprising faculty, staff, alumni, donors, and
students, among others.

**Trustees may well be underestimating
what they, themselves, can accomplish internally
without a national search firm being involved.**

Another question smaller, revenue-dependent colleges should be asking is whether it is really necessary to search the entire country for a candidate. Flying in dozens of candidates, even for airport interviews, can cost a fortune.

231

As there are several rounds of interviews, having too many candidates from afar can add tens of thousands of dollars that didn't have to be spent. It is hard to believe that a college in the East, for instance, is unable to find an ideal candidate from among the hundreds, and maybe even thousands, of colleges within a couple of hundred miles from them. 'National search' sounds impressive, but does it really make a difference that is worth the amount of money and time spent?

Breaking through the presidential ceiling is something that many will sacrifice anything to do. There are many stories known within the profession of chief academic officers from, say, California, who took a presidency on the east coast, or in the mid-west, in order to become a president. Then, within a year or two, they were busily at work trying to get back to California, or wherever their roots truly were, and eventually succeeded.

Trustees should also do their own reference checks, especially when the references are from other Trustees. This important task is typically conducted by the search firm. Especially in today's blogging world, it is increasingly more difficult to separate the wheat from the chaff, including the truth from rumor. Anyone who has been a college president is likely to have some people, perhaps many, who didn't think he/she did a particularly good job and such critics are likely to be more vocal and easier to find than those who are positive.

Trustees should do everything they can to 'own' the selection process.

The search committee should be advisory and not the final decision makers. To that end, the search committee shouldn't be called upon to vote or otherwise rank their favorites. Rather, they should submit a group of candidates they consider to be qualified and suited for the position in no particular order of preference.

While the President serves the entire college community and beyond, it is finally the Board of Trustees to whom the President reports. In that respect, no matter how much support the President may have garnered from a broader constituency, the Board should make the final decision and thereby select someone they believe they can work with, trust, support and champion.

Many Trustees, and others, have observed the typical lack of a succession protocol in higher education, which has proven to be more effective than not in providing relatively seamless transitions outside of higher education, most notably in (pardon the dirty word) corporations. While colleges sometimes have a potential successor in the wings, almost always the Provost, rarely is that person moved into the presidency when the vacancy occurs. At best, such an heir apparent is appointed interim president and folded into the year-long search, a time when the institution faces the prospect of little to no momentum. Other times, the successor isn't even the interim as that would be seen as an unfair advantage to his/her candidacy.

Higher education might well be much better served if such a succession model could replace the search-firm run 'national search' model that is presently in place. Some major universities have employed such internal succession systems to their great satisfaction. A notable case is New York University where NRY Provost Jay Oliva was long known to be the successor to John Brademus, and the transition was immediate and seamless. Then, when Jay Oliva retired, everyone knew that NYU Law School Dean John Sexton would similarly take over. There were no year-long periods of institutional limbo and inertia, and the successors picked up where their predecessors left off without redefining the future of the University to suit their new agenda.

Such as succession model is unlikely to emanate from smaller colleges because the greater community within the college, especially the faculty, will not likely go along with any change that is contrary to the model employed by the top national colleges and universities.

Were such a model to become a national standard, colleges would experience a lot less disruption during presidential transitions as a successor would take office almost immediately after his/her predecessor departed. Additionally, the new president would be a known entity that has, presumably, bought into the directions and policies that have been laid out by the Board. Too often, a new president arrives with an entirely new agenda calling upon the college to rethink most everything to conform to the visions of the new presidents. Sometimes, this is exactly what a troubled institution needs. Often, it isn't.

Where colleges would be best served, if it were doable, would be to avoid the year long limbo of the presidential search process that leaves many institutions inert at a time when they need to be dealing with issues that are pressing.

A succession plan would eliminate that problem.

Chapter 22

Strategic Plans

Just about every college, today, has something it calls a strategic plan. Regional accrediting agencies have come to require that such a document exists. There is nothing very unique or new about strategic plans except, perhaps, the name. Decades ago, such plans were called Management by Objectives (MBO's) along with many other variations. Today, though, strategic planning seems to be what it is all about.

In principle, there is nothing wrong with having a strategic plan and the accrediting agencies are spot on in calling upon colleges to have one. What passes for strategic planning, however, often falls far short of anything particularly useful to the institution. Surprisingly, though, many accrediting agencies do accept strategic plans that are sometimes not very strategic; as do Boards of Trustees.

Most fundamentally, strategic plans should focus on goals and aspirations, going forward, that provide a road map for everyone involved at the college. To that end, strategic plans are typically designed by committees with representatives from all constituencies including faculty, staff, students, alumni and, even, members of the community.

Metaphorically, committees are notorious for creating camels instead of horses, and strategic plans often become victim to the committee's diverse, and not atypically, romantic ideals. Where they too often fall short is when they are largely a list of wondrous adjectives that are impossible to monitor or measure.

Typical strategic goals can sound like the following:

- Be more competitive in attracting students with strong academic backgrounds

- Achieve a higher level of financial excellence

- Improve external support for the College

- Become more nationally visible

- Achieve greater diversity among students and staff

- Achieve continued renewal of the College

The above soliloquies and many other such aspirations like them become the generic underpinnings of too many strategic plans which can too often end up as a shopping list of platitudes covering virtually every special interest in advocacy at the College not unlike the annual Presidential State of the Union address to Congress.

What are missing in these plans are the strategies to achieve such aspirations and the specifics of the aspiration. Let's face it, virtually all enrollment-revenue driven colleges, for which this book is written:

- would welcome being less enrollment-revenue driven

- would welcome more students of higher academic ability who are better able to pay the costs of attending

- would welcome greater diversity

- would welcome more external support

- etc., etc., etc.

The fundamental template that most Colleges call their strategic plan is almost uniform. What each College then needs to do is put together a specific list of quantitatively measurable goals that can be monitored for progress toward a clear outcome. These goals also have to be prioritized, as it is impossible for Colleges to be all things to all people and to address all outstanding shortfalls simultaneously and/or with equal intensity.

Such measurable goals probably shouldn't be constructed by an egalitarian committee unfamiliar with the operational nuances of each functional area. It would be easy, for example, to have a committee unfamiliar with external support set a 'strategic' goal to raise an additional million dollars a year for scholarships. Any such 'strategic' goal set by those uninvolved in having to achieve the goal is, frankly, a worthless goal that won't be achieved.

Instead of being created by eclectic and diverse committees, strategic goals should be formulated by those who are going to be responsible for achieving the goal, then subject to negotiation and approval by the senior management of the College and then by the Board of Trustees.

So, if there is a need for, and a priority for, external sources of support, the Development personnel should be formulating a set of measurable goals that they believe they can achieve which should also explicitly outline what resources will be needed to achieve that goal, and how long it will take. In all probability, Development personnel are not going to want to make promises they don't believe they can likely achieve and this is where negotiation with senior management and the Board of Trustees comes in.

The same goes for virtually any other aspiration in any Strategic Plan. If better and more diverse students are sought, the Admissions personnel should be playing a lead role in developing goals along with, perhaps, the Faculty who need to be assessing the academic offerings and their relevance to consumer demand. Once again, the goals for improvement need to be quantified so everyone knows what is expected and how success or failure will be measured.

Student success also needs to be critically measurable, and too often is not. Faculty will typically establish goals for student outcomes that include aspirations like:

- Learn and apply skills in quantitative reasoning

- Learn and apply skills in critical thinking

- Learn to become good communicators

- Learn skills in information technology

- Pursue a broad-based liberal arts education

- Develop skills in inquiry and research

- Become responsible and engaged citizens

- And the list goes on. . .

Too many strategic plans cite unmeasurable ideals that are little more that idealistic clichés. What is missing, once again, is how these aspirations can be measured to ascertain that the college has indeed fulfilled its commitments and promises. Does just taking a course in communications and passing it thereby make a student a good communicator? What must each student successfully have accomplished to graduate a responsible and engaged citizen?

Not infrequently, strategic plans stop after the list of aspirations and ideals has been accumulated. Then, every few years a similarly diverse committee of college community constituents assembles to assess the state of the strategic plan without really having any way to explicitly measure whether anything has been accomplished. Those responsible for each area will submit some performance data that will hopefully cite positive outcomes but rarely is this being compared to specific measurements that had originally been set.

Well, we've done it!! Our year long strategic planning process is completed. We are hereby resolved to making the College as excellent as it can be and we further commit ourselves to preparing students for their future.

Thus, if everyone agrees that improved external support is a top priority that needs to be improved, a measurable goal first has to be agreed upon, especially by those who are going to be held responsible for the achievement of the goal. What kind of improvement is expected. . .exactly what kind? And by when? Once that is established, there should be an accompanying strategy (ergo, strategic plan) for exactly what needs to be done that hasn't been done in the past in order to achieve this presumably loftier goal. Trying harder, along with prayers, shouldn't be an acceptable strategy for success.

In the case of external support, the strategy may include new and additional effort from the president and the Board of Trustees, and might also include additional investments in resources and staffing. All that should be laid out in advance and accepted, or rejected, as part of the overall strategic plan.

Boards of Trustees can play a very valuable role by insisting that all strategic plan facets include specific measurable targets with timetables. Without such detail, there is no strategic plan.

In addition to specifics, all strategic plan goals, in order to be realistic and valid, have to

be linked to the actual budgets and resource capacities of the college or university.

Egalitarian strategic plan committees are prone to building an ideal dream that reaches far beyond the possible. . .especially what is feasible to accomplish within the time frames of the plan.

Such 'plans' are doomed to failure. Trustees need to be challenging each goal asking what will be needed, that isn't already budgeted, in order to achieve the goal. If those resources cannot be made available, the goal shouldn't be established no matter how wonderful it would be to achieve.

Chapter 23

"Corporate"
Needn't *Entirely* be a
Dirty Word

There will likely be critics of this book, including college presidents, provosts and professors, and probably their professional associations, who will go so far as to condemn it as wrongly promoting a corporate mentality in higher education, a criticism that is not infrequently attributed to Trustees. These critics will insist that higher education is not a commodity that should acquiesce to consumer demand and that Trustees should defer to the members of the Academy, namely the professoriate along with presidents and provosts, who can establish what is in the best interests of learning without regard to market forces. They will insist that the core value in education should always focus on the development of the person as a whole and, to achieve that mission, the Academy should never succumb to the 'ever present' presence of greed in the corporate mentality.

Such critics go so far as to lament what they see as the evolution of higher education job titles from deans to vice presidents as representing a corroding shift from the fundamental principles of higher education to the implicit negative motivations of corporations.

These same folks have long challenged any Trustee, especially those from business backgrounds, who raise the kinds of questions that this book encourages Trustees to be raising more often: Questions about revenue and cost that many in the Academy find counter-intuitive to their noble mission.

To the contrary, this book does not advocate that colleges and universities mirror corporations.

Higher education remains a largely not-for-profit entity and is probably best served to stay that way. Colleges and universities don't have to make a profit for owners or stockholders who seemingly can never make enough profit. Decisions in higher education don't have to be made based on how the most can be realized in profits for the least amount of investment. College and university presidents aren't faced with having to keep an eye on the price of their stock (nowadays, from hour to hour) and thereby make decisions almost solely on what will favorably influence the increased value of their stock. Unlike corporate CEO's, college presidents are not paid based on the amount of money they can squeeze out of the enterprise they oversee.

There is an enormous amount of freedom that is enjoyed by college presidents, provosts and professors that permits them to be making decisions and pursuing directions that are qualitative in nature and can be principally based on the pursuit of optimizing teaching and learning, and even research.

While this book may not be advocating mirroring corporate practices, the opposite extreme of seeing nothing that can be learned from corporations is probably not advisable either. To be sure, there is a lot of corporate culture motive that understandable sets a negative tone. The creators of mortgage-back securities and derivatives

247

made a fortune on the shoulders of world economic health. They probably deserve the distain the get and have added to the negatives of corporate motivations.

On the other hand, there are myriad examples of corporate innovation that just about everyone agrees has contributed to the quality of life while also making those improvements increasingly affordable.

Such examples can reach back a century or more when, for example, Henry Ford introduced the automobile assembly line thereby making the automobile affordable to the middle class while concurrently improving the product quality. More recently, Steve Jobs and Apple have revolutionized our lifestyles with extraordinary products that few would find objectionable and most would consider miraculous. Yes, both made a profit too, but that didn't prevent them from putting quality and accessibility at a high priority. What they did, and the way they went about it, can be a lesson for higher education worth consideration rather than being stereo-typed as corporate and therefore anti-intellectual.

Academics need to stop throwing out the babies with the dirty corporate bath water and be open to the notion that there can be what some experts call 'blended, integrated multi-sector skill sets' that would be advisable and a

potential solution to many challenges facing colleges.

College and universities simply cannot disregard the fact that they need money to pay the bills. For the 1,500 or so enrollment-revenue dependent colleges in America, that money is not guaranteed to them by a state government as is the case with the public universities that now enroll the majority of college and university students. To the contrary, the 1,500 smaller, unendowed, enrollment-revenue colleges in the US have no choice but to respect the realities of the marketplace and accommodate the most important priorities that the consuming public discern and seeks in the colleges they decide to select. Any college president, provost or professor refusing to 'lower themselves' to that reality is 'jumping off a bridge to prove the law of gravity,' and, in doing so, is seriously jeopardizing the very survival of the college with which they are associated.

Scholars are welcome to continue their pursuit of higher education's core values, but Trustees have to be certain that such academics are not so idealistically motivated that they refuse to adapt their pursuits in ways that will stimulate the interest of the (pardon the dirty word) 'paying customers' that every enrollment-revenue college simply cannot forgo. A college might well have the very best academic program that has ever been imagined, but if no one wants to pay for that very best program, something else that can be (pardon the dirty word) 'sold' needs to take its place.

As long as enrollment-revenue dependent colleges continue to need money to pay their bills, those same colleges cannot ignore the realities of the marketplace regardless of the ideals they may cherish.

Trustees need to stand their ground and demand what is necessary to insure that the college survives.

While there may be wide-reaching advocacy for shared governance, **the Board stands alone, legally-speaking, in bearing the fiduciary responsibility to insure the fiscal stability of the institution.** Trustees are also legally bound to insure that the college is fulfilling its contractual obligation to the students and their families who are paying a lot of money with the rightful expectation that they are receiving what they are being told they will get from their education. When something goes wrong, all the participants in shared governance will not be the subject of a lawsuit. The Trustees, along with the CEO, will be in the spotlight and will be held liable. Thus, they cannot walk away from their responsibilities without greatly jeopardizing their liability.

Hopefully, Trustees working in partnership with the President and senior offers can also find ways to enable a spirit of shared governance.

The fact is that nothing will succeed at a college where the faculty, the provost and the president are rowing in contrary directions . . . even if and when that direction is for a Heavenly cause...which, unfortunately, too many of the most financially inadvisable causes often represent.

Chapter 24

In Closing

Presidential-Board Symbiosis is Essential

S ome college presidents, if they have read the book to this point, may well have groaned now and then troubled that their Trustees, upon reading this book, will be incited to make their jobs as chief executives that much more difficult. Hopefully, not that many presidents came to that conclusion, but if any did they have wrongly misunderstood the intent of the authors.

252

As was stated in the opening paragraphs and echoed throughout the book, **there is no intended message to Trustees that they more actively involve themselves in the micromanagement of the institution.** To the contrary, such meddling will hurt the college and deplete the effectiveness of the president and his/her management team.

No college or university, or corporation, or organization of any kind, including government, can optimize its effectiveness when the governing body overseeing it is at cross purposes with the executives managing it.

If there was ever a good example of how dysfunctional such relationships can become, one need look no further than the current state of affairs in the U.S. federal government where the President and Congress have, in the views of many, brought constructive government to a virtual halt that has created one fiscal cliff after another.

No college or university is any different when it comes to the importance of Presidents and Boards working on behalf of each other, meaning Boards that are committed to the success of their President and his/her management team. Any indication that the Board and the President are not on the same boat, rowing in the same direction, to a common destination, will be the Achilles' Heel of that institution which bodes ominous for any prospect of success.

Colleges and universities are, by nature, communities of diverse and often conflicting ideologies. There are few jobs more demanding, and second guessed, than that of the college president. Like US presidents, who are doing very well when 60% of the public are supportive and positive, college presidents are similarly faced with constituencies that are all over the map ideologically.

When that community sees a Board that is not supporting its President, or vice versa, the likelihood of institutional chaos is greatly amplified.

The point of this book, in that respect, is to help Trustees understand the problems and challenges typical of revenue-dependent colleges in the early decades of the 21st century. Never have the challenges been more daunting. Like never before, Boards of Trustees have to understand the fundamentals if they are going to be part of the solution instead of contributing to the problem.

We would like this book to increase the incidence of the former (i.e., solutions), and to that end hope that a better awareness of vital signs and red flags will strengthen the Trustee role in an increasing number of success stories.

As echoed many times, this book is not calling upon Trustees to take the law into their own hands. Trustees, and especially the Chairman in partnership with the President, have to back the President and let the President do the very difficult job that he/she was appointed by the Trustees to do. On the other hand, though, Trustees are not helping if they are rubber stamping issues they don't understand. And they are not contributing if they are nodding their heads in unison to presentations.

Trustees need to be asking challenging questions based on their clear understanding of the challenges facing the institution they are overseeing. Presidents needn't be and shouldn't be alarmed by such overtures. To the contrary, they should welcome such intelligent and well-intended involvement.

In the end, the success stories will be at those institutions where Presidents and their Boards believe in each other, and symbiotically work together with the genuine desire for each other's success.

Chapter 25

Recapping Vital Signs

A ny reader, who upon getting to this concluding section of the book, has sensed that Trustees have been given a green light to micro-manage the college or university they oversee has missed an important introductory caveat. From the opening chapter, Trustees were warned. . .

If it isn't broken, Don't fix it.

Any trustee reading this book who can cite their college as enjoying a strong fiscal foundation, with a full undergraduate enrollment, resulting in a high retention and graduation rate, while maintaining a manageable discounting rate, and also enjoying a flourishing fund raising program, which contributes to a widely-regarded academic program with up-to-date campus and educational resources. . .should leave well enough alone. In such cases, the president, senior officers and faculty obviously have the situation well under control and everything is ticking like a Swiss watch. Such Trustees can put this book on the shelf and hope they never need to refer to it. In doing so, Trustees should look for every way in which they can assure that their very competent management team never wants to move on.

Rather, this book is designed to help Trustees deal with colleges that are not flourishing: where enrollments are falling short, where discounting keeps eating into needed enrollment revenues, where campus resources are losing ground, where gifts are falling short of what is needed, where budgets are becoming harder to balance, etc. In such cases, something is wrong and what is wrong may not be obvious. For such situations, this book is hopefully a useful tool that provides some ideas of where Trustees might search for answers and solutions by, first, understanding where problems typically lie and, then, at least having some questions to ask management that may help reveal problems. As one old saying goes, locating the problem is 50% of the solution.

Here, then, is a quick compendium of key vital signs covered in the book along with some specific questions that will hopefully provide Trustees with a starting point.

Admissions

Enrollment revenue is central to the success or failure of all tuition-dependent institutions. Any struggling institution should look here first and begin by asking the following questions:

1. **Inquiries/Prospects.** If prospects are 'up,' and enrollments are not, the source of such prospects needs to be scrutinized. If lists were bought from testing services and those names were added to the prospect column, prospects aren't really 'up' as many-to-most of those names are never going to turn into interested applicants. If such names are coming from admissions fairs, they are almost as worthless. The only really promising increases in this area are when the names are unsolicited and coming from interested students who have learned about the college and are drawn to it.

2. **Applications.** If applications are 'up,' but don't turn into comparable enrollments, was the application fee waived? Did computer based 'common applications' contribute? Were admissions application requirements 'relaxed'? All such stimulants could lead to a surge in applications that are unlikely to come from students who will enroll.

3. **Admits.** If admits aren't turning into enrollments, how many of the admits had SAT's and GPA's that were below the national average scores? How many students indicated that the college was a first choice for them?

4. **Deposits.** If fewer than 25% of those students admitted deposited, what happened to the other 75%? Obviously, they opted for another college, but why?

5. **Enrolled.** If fewer than 85% of those students who deposited didn't finally enroll, what happened? If the deposit was refundable, then, obviously, many of the deposits weren't all that committed. Did another school make a counteroffer that drew them away?

Financial Aid/Discounting

1. If discounting is in excess of 40%, too much enrollment income is being written off.

2. What were the discount rates offered by category and how many students in each category were offered that rate?

3. What was the average discount rate offered as compared to the average discount rate of those students who accepted the admit offer? If the yield on admits had a substantially higher discount rate than the average on offer to admits, the wrong students are declining the admit offer and too many of the wrong students are accepting the offer.

4. What is the net FTE of students enrolled as compared to the gross FTE? The difference is the total of students attending for nothing.

Branding/Niche

1. What do you believe is the college's niche? If the only distinctions you know are qualitative, related to characteristics like 'excellence,' then your college doesn't have a distinctive and magnetic niche.

2. Does the college website showcase successful recent alumni/ae?

3. Does the college website profile exemplary faculty where it is easy to find them?

4. Does the college website showcase currently enrolled students who are on-track connecting to post-graduate placements either in graduate school or in a profession related to their major? Does the college website present examples of recent graduates and what they are doing after graduation?

First Year Indicators

1. If more than 15% of first year students don't return for the sophomore year, something is wrong. Why did they leave?

2. Each freshman who doesn't return is the virtual equivalent of a 75% refund on a sale that was made. On average, that comes to about $80,000 per lost freshman. What happened?

3. How is the freshman year proving to be the most invested program at the college? Or not at all?

Administrative Staffing

1. Has senior administrative staffing grown disproportionately to the other operating costs of the college?

2. Smaller colleges shouldn't have administrative staffs comparable to large universities. Any college with fewer than 3,000 students but with a Chief of Staff is a likely example for excessive and unnecessary administrative costs. What is the Chief of Staff doing that can't be done by the President and the Vice Presidents for Administration and Finance?

3. Public and media relations are often overspent in smaller colleges with limited media interest. What are the measurable outcomes that justify this kind of expense?

Bricks, Mortar & Ivy

1. Have Trustees visited those colleges cited as successful competitors?

2. The campus visit has long been cited as the single most influential factor in prospective student college choice. What effect does the campus have on visitors? How is that favorably influencing applications and first choice decision?

3. Trustees should have visited at least 3 or 4 other colleges cited as 'cross-application' schools by the admissions office. Is this the case?

Assessing Faculty

1. How many students does each faculty member have in the total number of classes being taught each semester? This is not an across the board average, but grouped by those with ten or fewer students per semester, to those teaching over 100.

2. How many professors teach five days a week, four days a week, three days a week, fewer than three days?

263

3. How many full-time professors teach no freshman courses?

4. Are full-time faculty paid extra for teaching, and other institutional work, that occurs outside the 30-week span of the fall and spring semesters?

5. How evenly distributed are student advising loads? Do the most enrolled majors have trouble finding a faculty advisor in their discipline?

Assessing Instructional Costs

1. How many majors have fewer than 2 dozen students in each of the junior and senior years?

2. How many majors have fewer than three full-time faculty in the discipline?

3. What is the faculty student ratio in each of the advised majors?

Fund Raising

1. Are the costs of fund raising more than 25% of what is actually raised each year?

2. Do the President and Board take the lead in cultivating major donor prospects?

3. Is there a financial advisor working with older alumni to set up charitable trusts that are irrevocable, providing the alum with a better rate of return while offering the college a guaranteed bequest?

Library & Technology

1. Is there any monitoring of books that are virtually never used?

2. Is there any attempt to scrutinize the advisability of stocking reference books that students rarely use?

3. Who decides what new books will be acquired, and not?

4. Is there any part of the campus that is not fully wireless for Internet accessibility?

5. Are all classrooms computer friendly?

6. Is there any student feedback system that documents their assessment of technological resources available, and unavailable to them?

7. Is there any program to 'train' faculty to become more computer literate in their teaching?

8. Can students register for courses on line?

9. Can all students be readily contacted via Internet, and by SMS text, including for emergencies?

10. Is there a regular communication to student families via Internet?

Strategic Planning

1. Does the strategic plan have goals that can be quantitatively measured? Specifically, goals should not be cited qualitatively with words like 'improve,' 'upgrade,' 'strengthen,' unless accompanied by an explanation of exactly how that 'improvement, etc.' will be evaluated as having 'improved.'

2. Does the strategic plan have deadlines for milestones to be accomplished?

3. Do the goals align with the needs of the institution?

4. If these goals require additional investments in resources, what exactly is the price of those investments and how will the outcome justify, and for that matter, ultimately fund the cost of the investment?

5. Does the manager responsible for the goal believe it can be achieved?

6. Has the long range financial plan been designed to align with the strategic goals? If so, do the financial planners believe the financial plan is realistic?

Presidential Searches

1.   Do we really need to conduct a national search, or can we not limit our reach to a more regional process that will reduce costs and perhaps yield someone more comfortable and familiar with the College's surrounding culture?

2.   If we seek someone with a successful track record of prior leadership experience, can we find a way to modify the search process in a way that guarantees confidentiality throughout the process and thereby

doesn't deter sitting presidents from being candidates?

3. Many of the candidates that would be ideal for the College are not necessarily interested in leaving the presidency they now enjoy. Should we consider approaching such presidents in confidence and attempting to recruit them?

4. Do we really need a search firm? Would it not be better if we conducted our own reference checks? Are not Trustees who know the candidates more likely to be candid with fellow Trustees than they are with search firm executives?

The cartoons appearing
from time to time
in this book
were conceived
and drawn
by
Norman Smith